Turbo Pascal Library

Turbo Pascal® Library

Douglas S. Stivison

SYBEX®

Berkeley • Paris • Düsseldorf • London

Book design by Joe Roter

Library of Congress Card Number: 86-60567
ISBN 0-89588-330-9
Printed by Haddon Craftsmen
Manufactured in the United States of America
10 9 8 7 6 5 4 3 2 1

For my wife,
Heather

ACKNOWLEDGMENTS

In many ways, it is more difficult to acknowledge one's debts in a second book than in the first, because you become aware of just how many people are involved in the creation and production of a book.

The largest debt must go to my wife, Heather, who has now put up with our home life turned upside-down in order to meet publication deadlines. Without her commitment and encouragement—and certainly without her assuming my household and parenting tasks—the book could never have been written. Similarly, my daughter Megan has been a very good sport about having her playtime with Dad preempted by writing chores.

I also need to thank the many readers of my earlier book, *Introduction to Turbo Pascal,* for their comments, suggestions and encouragement. Many readers of that book said that it genuinely helped them become Turbo programmers, and these words of thanks and encouragement provided the sustaining motivation to complete the present book.

Few of the programs in this book are entirely my own creation. Overwhelmingly they combine routines, ideas, procedures, functions, tricks, and suggestions from hundreds of programs found on bulletin boards, in other books, swapped at club meetings, in magazine articles, or adapted from other languages. In most cases, it is impossible to acknowledge the original sources, but any programmers who find their own "great ideas" appearing in these pages without attribution should be assured that I do not claim credit for any of the brilliance or cleverness of many of these programs. I merely collected, tested, refined, and tried to document and make consistent ideas gathered from others.

Although computer bulletin boards are often represented in the popular press as tools for mischief-bent, teenage hackers, the majority of boards are run as labors of love by individuals sincerely interested in the exchange of programming ideas. I have been a frequent user of many boards, and I would like to thank a few system operators (SYSOPs) who have been extraordinarily helpful.

The best Turbo bulletin board in America is run by Dave Carroll, who also happens to be one of the best computer writers in America. He has been a consistent source of good ideas. Chuck Childers of the wonderful Warehouse bulletin board in Ohio has also been consistently helpful and encouraging. Bob Klahn and Van Olmstead both operate FIDO boards in Delaware and both have not only been helpful technically, but have been most hospitable hosts as well. There are many other boards that I have used from time to time, and I wish to thank the other SYSOPs who I have not yet had to pleasure to get to know.

Of course, there is also the crew at SYBEX who helped to develop this title, edit it, and produce the finished book (and then take care of all the follow-up inquiries). Jim Compton was the editor, Dan Tauber the technical reviewer, Dave Clark and Olivia Shinomoto the word processors, Donna Scanlon the typesetter, and Laura Hurd the proofreader. Let me just say thank you to one and all, and fully acknowledge that this book is truly a team effort.

Finally, it is impossible to separate my Turbo writing from my other professional obligations. Working for an international corporation in the high-tech field must be one of the most exciting jobs in the world today. There is a special feeling working with talent that transcends linguistic, national and job-classification boundaries. Specifically, I must acknowledge the inspiration of my colleagues in the Federal Republic of Germany and in the United Kingdom, who form one of the most innovative and creative teams in the entire world of composition technology. My thanks go to Knut Schmeidel, Bernd Holthusen, Rudy Meisner, Reiner Ter and Roland Zirn in West Germany; and Richard Beer, Bill Tucker, and Neil Goldsworthy in the United Kingdom for their contribution to a truly heady atmosphere of excellence. I must acknowledge the palpable, "can-do" excitement generated by all the members of the nascent Scangraphic team in the United States. I would also like to specifically name Denis M. Collura, who has had the fundamental vision, courage, leadership and perseverance through adversity to make it all happen.

TABLE OF CONTENTS

INTRODUCTION

Why This Book Was Written

My earlier book, *Introduction to Turbo Pascal,* was written "to help readers develop, as quickly as possible, the ability to write problem-solving programs in Turbo Pascal." From the response I have had from readers, it seems to have done exactly that, helping many readers overcome the initial hurdles in getting their first Turbo programs to run.

Over 400,000 copies of Turbo Pascal have been sold and there has been a flood of Turbo-related commercial products. Literally thousands of users are checking into the Turbo bulletin boards around the country, hundreds of schools now use Turbo for teaching, and with the signing of the formal agreement whereby IBM will sell Turbo, it is obvious that the number of Turbo users is growing and will continue to grow enormously. Inevitably, then, there is a need for a library of useful routines, procedures, functions, and programs written in Turbo to help both novice and intermediate Turbo programmers expand their repertoires of programming tricks. There is a need for a "cookbook" of routines that can be used by themselves, combined with others, modified, or merely studied.

This book was written to serve all of these needs.

What Kind of Programs Are in This Book?

This book covers useful extensions to Turbo, including some functions—familiar to programmers with experience in other languages—that seem to have been overlooked in Turbo. These include the ability to get the system time and date and to raise a number to any power.

Routines range from the almost trivially obvious (but still valuable) to the moderately complex. Understandability, even more than optimum efficiency, has been the primary goal.

Some routines will serve as models for your own customized code in doing common programming tasks, such as printing user messages and soliciting user response. In one form or another these operations appear in almost all programs, and sooner or later we all develop our favorite ways of doing them.

There are also routines to provide some handy system-related functions, such as getting directories and opening, copying, listing, and killing files.

In addition to these building blocks, the book contains some ready-to-run programs including games and the ubiquitous mortgage amortization program.

You will find handy tools for common, but tricky occurrences. For example, one of the shortcomings of the mailing list program in *Introduction to Turbo Pascal* was that there was no easy way to get a directory of files while running the program. A user had to exit the program and use operating system commands to view a directory and to kill unwanted files. The *Directry* and *Delete* functions in this book were developed specifically as an extension to the needs of users of the earlier program. I'm sure many of you have currently working programs that could benefit from extensions like these.

What Is Not Here

This book does not have monstrously long programs. Although Turbo has defied the critics in its overall speed and ease of use, many traditionalists have categorized Turbo as only useful for programs of "trivial" size. Many amateur-written graphics, scientific, and communications programs are extremely ambitious and, like several commercial products, attest to the ability to write excellent Turbo programs running to 50,000 lines of code. Just take a look at the PIBTERM program on the bulletin boards to see how complex a programming task can be addressed by Turbo.

Unfortunately, as much as the author would like to refute the claims that Turbo is only suitable for trivial tasks, a book of this size and scope is not a practical forum for the debate. There are no programs in the book that run more than a few pages.

Similarly, however cleverly tasks can be accomplished through the use of in-line machine code and the very low-level manipulation of computer ports and interrupts, these topics are best left to a more advanced book for programmers who already have a solid understanding of computer internals and assembly-language programming.

How the Programs Are Done

Every program that is really a tool has a companion "TestXX" procedure to demonstrate its operation. There are literally thousands of clever routines floating around, but without documentation and without some way to exercise them, they are almost unusable. I hope that each of these test procedures will show at least one good way that the tool can be used.

For example, there is a routine (*YesOrNo* in the include file ROUTINE.INC) that paints a screen message and accepts a response. Its use is not intuitive, but the accompanying *TestYesOrNo* procedure shows exactly what the routine does. These test procedures should reduce the need for detailed explanation.

Along with these demonstrations of the program operation, I have consistently used the most informative identifiers possible. On one hand, this practice violates one of the principles of good programming—not to waste space. On the other hand, when a Turbo program is compiled, long identifiers do not take up any more memory than short ones. As a result, they help to make the program operation clear without any sacrifice in execution speed or program size (as would be the case with languages such as BASIC). Thus I have chosen to use very long identifiers (such as *NameOfFileToBeDeleted*) rather than shorter ones (such as *FName*) to make the programs self-documenting.

An extension of this philosophy has been that many of the procedures serve mainly to make programs more understandable. Thus I use a procedure called *Beep* to sound the computer buzzer rather than the equally effective, but completely cryptic statement

```
WRITELN (#07)
```

Similarly, in several programs I have broken procedures into even smaller, informatively-named procedures simply to make the operation of the larger procedure more understandable. In the Turbo directory program, for example, rather than one procedure I used several small procedures (*SetUpDOS, DecodeDirectoryEntry, DetermineMask, CallDOS*) simply to make the operation of the directory procedure more obvious.

Yet there is always the temptation to explain too much. In some programs—particularly those using calls to the MS/PC-DOS operating system—I leave the system-level operations only lightly annotated. The programs will work well as-is. For more information on these operating-system calls, look in the documentation that comes with your operating system.

Hardware and Software Requirements

Turbo Pascal is available in versions (or "implementations") for most of today's personal computers. Differences between these versions are relatively minor, but they can be significant enough to prevent a program written for one version from running properly on another. The most important differences involve those commands that call functions specific to a particular operating system.

The most popular implementation of Turbo Pascal is for the MS/PC-DOS operating system, used on the IBM PC computers (PC-DOS) and the "IBM-compatibles" made by other manufacturers (MS-DOS), and it is assumed that readers of this book are using that version. An effort has been made to identify those lines of code that would have to be changed for a given program to run on the CP/M operating system.

Sources of These Programs—and Further Exploration

Many of the programs in this book are amalgamations or adaptations of programs gleaned from a wide range of sources, including the Turbo Users Group, magazine articles, published books, and personal experimentation. Most of the ideas and techniques came from several other Sybex books and the plethora of programs appearing on Turbo bulletin boards.

Computer bulletin boards are a tremendous source of good ideas. However, using them requires a huge effort in separating the good from the worthless. The code on most boards, although a limitless source of other peoples' ideas, is written by programmers of widely varying degrees of skill. Moreover, most programs are (at best) cryptically documented, and a certain amount of code simply does not work. Thus the programs in this book are the distillation of a tremendous amount of trial, error, modification, and experimentation. The finished programs reflect a fortune in telephone connect time and months of all-night hacking sessions. But more importantly, they represent the actual ingenuity of hundreds of people I cannot even identify, much less say that I have met.

I would like to single out one particular source of good ideas. *Apple Pascal Games*, by Douglas Hergert and Joseph T. Kalash (SYBEX, 1981) has become the undisputed wellspring of game implementations in Pascal—regardless of dialect. Most of the games in this book—as well as most of the Pascal games to be found anywhere—are modeled on the programs contained in *Apple Pascal Games*. Until the definitive book of Turbo Pascal games is written, this remains the best inspiration.

1 Building Blocks

Introduction

One of the greatest strengths of Turbo Pascal is the ease with which it lends itself to modular structures. The most complex of programs can always be broken down into small, easily understood, easily debugged individual procedures and functions. The process of attacking even the most ambitious programming task is further aided by the tremendous flexibility that Turbo gives you in creating identifiers—both for variables and for procedures and functions—that convey information and help to make the operation of a program clear to anyone reading its listing.

Once you have a general algorithm for solving a problem in Turbo, the task of creating a working program is essentially one of selecting appropriate data structures to reflect the real-world organization of the information to be manipulated and then creating and assembling the individual modules to process the data.

Although Turbo offers an extraordinary array of predefined procedures and functions to do a great deal of work, one soon discovers that there are always certain "missing commands" that would make one's programming life easier. These operations can range from fetching and interpreting keyboard input—used in virtually every program—to something specific to your particular programming tasks. For example, I work with German, British, and American engineers involved with the design and use of a line of typesetting equipment. Thus, I am constantly converting values expressed in inches, in millimeters, and in the picas and points used by printers. While it does not make sense for the creators of Turbo to add a stock function (like ORD, STR, or TRUNC) to perform such conversions, they figure into several programs a week in this line of work. It also does not make sense for me to write the conversion routines again and again. The sensible solution, then, was to create a group of routines to perform these functions. Collected into one "include" file, they can be added to my programs as needed. (To learn how to incorporate include files into programs, see *Introduction to Turbo Pascal.*) A version of them appears in this book in the *METRIC.PAS* program.

Whether or not you need to perform these particular conversions, the important point here is that I have actually customized the Turbo language to help address my everyday projects. You can do the same thing, regardless of your specific applications.

Turbo has proven that it is a serious programming language as opposed to a hacker's novelty and there are now both commercial and public-domain collections of procedures that address a huge range of programming situations. Today you can find collections of routines to expand Turbo for different industry-specific applications. In preparing this book, I investigated collections of procedures for engineering and high-precision mathematical applications, probability and statistical analysis, graphic manipulation, financial and actuarial calculations, and control of external sensing and analog-to-digital mechanisms.

Sources for many of these routines and others are listed in the Appendix to this book, so that with a little bit of investigation you can avoid having to reinvent the wheel for many of your specific programming needs.

Common to all Turbo programmers is the need not for job-specific extensions to Turbo but for a collection of routines that can simplify almost any programming task. The collection of routines presented in this chapter is a sampling of these kinds of tools. The chapter could easily have been ten times the size it is; but these twenty routines illustrate the basic concept of collecting routines into include files. Probably every reader will choose to discard some of the routines here and certainly will want to add some personal favorites. All readers will want to fine-tune the examples here to suit their own programming styles.

The modules in this chapter fall into four basic groups, according to the type of task they perform: making program listings more informative for the benefit of the original and follow-on programmer, standardizing user interaction from program to program, supplying the Turbo commands that programmers used to other languages might miss, and finally, making finished programs look more professional.

General-Purpose Routines—ROUTINE.INC and ROUTINE.PAS

We begin creating our library with a collection of general-purpose routines. This is the include file *ROUTINE.INC*, listed in Figure 1.1. Along with *ROUTINE.INC* is its driver program, *ROUTINE.PAS*, listed in Figure 1.2. As noted in the Introduction, most of the routines presented in this book are accompanied by such driver programs. Here, as elsewhere, the purpose is to allow you to see for yourself how the routines operate. This demonstration, along with the internal documentation provided in the form of comments and descriptive identifiers, to a great extent obviates the need for a line-by-line explication. Nonetheless, some items in each program will merit particular attention.

One such item here is the use of the user-created data type *UniversalString*. Because Turbo generates an error message when passing strings of unequal length between program modules, the "quick and dirty" expedient of declaring a 255-character-long string in the include file goes a long way to making these routines as general as possible. This is the reason for the lines:

```
TYPE
    UniversalString = STRING [255];
VAR
    Phrase : UniversalString;
```

Knowing that I have this definition in the include file, I make frequent use of variables of the type *UniversalString* in my specific application programs.

Beep, *Inc*, and *Dec* are all simple routines that do not actually save any lines of coding but simply add clarity to the program listing. *Inc* and *Dec* just increment and decrement a counter by one. *Beep* merely sounds the computer beeper; but it is more meaningful to someone reading a listing than its equivalent:

```
WRITELN (#7);
```

and more efficient than declaring in every program:

```
CONST
    Beep = #7; {Control G sounds beeper}
```

UpString is a very commonly used routine that saves tedious repetitive coding. It is a string-oriented version of the standard function UPCASE, in that it converts any string of legal length to all uppercase alphabetic characters while avoiding any problems trying to capitalize nonalphabetic characters (numbers and punctuation) embedded in the string. It makes keyboard-reading routines "user friendly" by accepting either uppercase or lowercase responses. The user does not have to be concerned with the status of the Caps and Caps-lock keys when typing responses.

Play offers an alternative to *Beep* by generating not just a beep but a tone of any specified pitch and duration. By passing different values to the procedure, you can add interesting sound effects to games, provide different tones to signal valid and invalid responses to prompts, and even play songs. It is used as part of a separate routine, *Canada,* to play a short tune.

The *Canada* routine was developed as a pleasant way to signal the completion of time-consuming processes. For example, a mailing list program developed for *Introduction to Turbo Pascal* can take several minutes to alphabetize a long list. There is no need for the user to hover about the computer during this time. When the sorting process is done, the program uses the Canada routine—rather than the more mundane computer beeper—to alert the operator that the task is done. Of course, you can modify the procedure to play almost any tune. "O Canada" was chosen simply because the author was first introduced to the art of making music on a computer by a talented programmer in Saskatoon, Saskatchewan many years ago.

Dup, Left, Right, and *Center* are used to place characters or text in specific locations. To a large extent they are typical of dozens of different variations on ways to supply a Turbo approximation of the TAB command in BASIC. *Dup* simply takes a character and creates a string containing the requested number of copies of the same character. It is a useful tool for printing lines of asterisks across the screen or page of listings. *Left* takes a string and simply prints it beginning at the left side of a field of the stated width. The related *Right* and *Center* routines take a string and append the appropriate number of spaces to the string to print it out either centered or right-justified in a field of the stated width. These modules use the *Dup* routine to add the needed spaces.

Power simply takes a real number and raises it to any power (expressed as an integer). It is not designed to accept negative exponents. It is included here simply to show a mathematical routine. Depending on the needs of your application, you could design a generic routine like this to determine average or mean values, convert between metric and English units or between Celsius and Fahrenheit, figure compound interest, or do just about any other repetitive calculation.

Date and *Time* are convenient routines for printing time and date stamps on printouts or making on-screen menus look more professional. They supply two more of Turbo's "missing" commands, TIME$ and DATE$, that BASIC programmers have come to expect.

These routines are important for several reasons. First, while they use Turbo's INTR, MSDOS, HI, and LO procedures, all of which involve access to operating-system calls, they illustrate that by taking a "cookbook" approach, the programmer not versed in the intricacies of his computer's operating system can use the procedures as-is to get the required functionality. You do not have to know about—or care—how DOS stores what value in what register in response to either a BIOS or a BDOS call or interrupt.

These routines are also important because, if you do decide to learn a bit more about these extremely powerful capabilities, you can modify the routines to let you set the time and date as well as read the current values. Even more ambitiously, you can create your own selective directory program, or clock program. Variations on these routines provide the basis for the program timer used in *TIMER.INC* and in the directory program shown in *DIRECTRY.PAS*.

User Interaction

Although several of the preceding routines deal with aspects of interacting with the program user, the next two routines are designed to optimize the process of communicating with the person who finally uses your finished Turbo programs. They are among the ones I use most frequently, and you will see them used in the majority of the programs in the remainder of this book.

WaitForAnyKey is the essence of simplicity, yet its use makes any program more professional. As its informative name suggests, the routine asks the user to strike any key to continue. Thus, it is useful for clearing the screen of title and instruction frames when the program user is finished reading them rather than after an arbitrary delay period. It is also useful for pausing between operations in programs that loop (say, playing each round of Blackjack or computing a different mortgage table). Why write this routine a hundred times, when it could be sitting in your toolbox?

YesOrNo is another time-saver with many applications. It accepts a prompting inquiry from the calling program ("Do you want to continue?" "Is the lineprinter turned on?" or "Play again?" for example) and awaits a response. It filters out erroneous responses and accepts upper- or lowercase input. Furthermore, it returns a Boolean value of TRUE if the user responds affirmatively. Thus the function can be used as a trigger for further action, as in this general example:

```
IF (YesOrNo) THEN DO Something
```

Operation

These are just a sampling of what you can do with collections of routines. Run the *ROUTINE.PAS* program shown in Figure 1.2, to see how the individual routines are used and how they operate. Incidentally, when you create your own libraries, it is always a good idea to write a short driver program to test your include files and make sure that they work as you expect before causing possibly unpredictable results in your larger projects.

```
{include file called Routine.inc}

TYPE
  UniversalString  = STRING [255];
VAR
  Phrase : UniversalString;

PROCEDURE Beep;
 {Simply a way to sound beeper--makes your code more self-
  descriptive}
BEGIN
  WRITELN (#07)
END;

PROCEDURE Inc (VAR I : INTEGER);         {Acts like INCR command
                                          in BASIC.}
BEGIN
  I := I + 1
END;

PROCEDURE Dec (VAR I : INTEGER);          {Companion TO Inc}
BEGIN
  I := I - 1;
END;

FUNCTION UpString (Words : UniversalString) : UniversalString;

{This function accepts a string made up of any combination of
 upper- and lowercase characters and returns the entire
 string in all uppercase.  It is a handy routine to make any
 parser more robust.  It illustrates a simple use of the
 existing UPCASE command.}

VAR
  I : INTEGER;
  LowerCaseAlphabet : SET OF CHAR;
BEGIN
  LowerCaseAlphabet := ['a'..'z'];
  FOR I := 1 TO LENGTH (Words) DO
    IF Words[I] IN LowerCaseAlphabet THEN Words[I] := UPCASE (Words[I]);
  UpString := Words
END;

PROCEDURE Play (Note, Time : INTEGER);
 {Used like Beep and also to play real tunes. Gives control over
  both pitch and duration of sound.}
BEGIN
  SOUND (Note);
  DELAY (Time);
  NOSOUND
END;

PROCEDURE Canada;
CONST
  Q = 300; {Quarter-note}
  H = 600;
  T = 900;
  W = 1200;
```

Figure 1.1: The collection of useful routines in the include file ROUTINE.INC.

```
    LowC = 262; {Portion of scale}
    D = 294;
    E = 330;
    F = 350;
    G = 392;
    A = 440;
  {Plays four bars of "O Canada" simply by calling Canada
   routine.  Useful to alert operator to the completion of long process.}
  BEGIN
    Play (E, H);
    Play (G, H);
    Play (G, Q);
    Play (LowC, T);
    Play (D, Q);
    Play (E, Q);
    Play (F, Q);
    Play (G, Q);
    Play (A, Q);
    Play (D, W)
  END;


  FUNCTION Dup (HowMany : INTEGER; WhatSymbol : CHAR) : UniversalString;
  VAR
    Temp : UniversalString;   {Holds pattern as it is created.}
    I    : BYTE;              {For Counter}
  BEGIN
    Temp := '';
    FOR I := 1 TO HowMany DO
      Temp := Temp + WhatSymbol;
    Dup := Temp
  END;


  FUNCTION Left (Phrase : UniversalString;
                 Width : INTEGER) : UniversalString;
  BEGIN
    IF LENGTH (Phrase) > Width THEN
      Left := COPY (Phrase, 1, Width)
    ELSE
      Left := Phrase + Dup (Width - LENGTH (Phrase),' ')
  END;

  FUNCTION Right (Phrase : UniversalString;
                  Width : INTEGER) : UniversalString;
  BEGIN
    IF LENGTH (Phrase) > Width THEN
      Right := COPY (Phrase, 1, Width)
    ELSE
      Right :=  Dup (Width - LENGTH (Phrase),' ') + Phrase
  END;


  FUNCTION Center (Phrase : UniversalString;
                   Width : INTEGER) : UniversalString;
  VAR
    LeftSpaces : BYTE;
```

Figure 1.1: (continued)

```
BEGIN
  IF (LENGTH (Phrase) > Width) THEN Center := Phrase
  ELSE
    BEGIN
     LeftSpaces := (Width - LENGTH (Phrase)) DIV 2;
     Center :=  Dup (LeftSpaces,' ') + Phrase
    END;
END; {If}

FUNCTION Power (Mantissa : REAL; Exponent : INTEGER): REAL;
VAR
  I    : INTEGER; {Counter}
  Temp : REAL;    {Temporary results}
BEGIN
  Temp := 1.0;
  FOR I := 1 TO Exponent DO
    Temp := Temp * Mantissa;
  Power := Temp
END;

FUNCTION Date: UniversalString; {Gets and decodes time from DOS.}
TYPE
  Registers = RECORD
              AX, BX, CX, DX, BP, SI, DS, ES, Flags : INTEGER;
            END;
VAR
  RegisterRecord : Registers;  {needed for any MSDOS call}
  Month          : STRING[9];
  Day            : STRING[2];
  Year           : STRING[4];
  DX,CX          : INTEGER;

BEGIN
  RegisterRecord.AX := $2A00; {AX register includes hex 2A: DOS
                               function to get date.}
  INTR ($21, RegisterRecord); {Hex $21 is the DOS interrupt for
                               many functions.}
  WITH RegisterRecord DO
  BEGIN
    STR (CX, Year);
    STR (LO (RegisterRecord.DX), Day);
    CASE  (HI (RegisterRecord.DX)) OF
      1 : Month := 'January';
      2 : Month := 'February';
      3 : Month := 'March';
      4 : Month := 'April';
      5 : Month := 'May';
      6 : Month := 'June';
      7 : Month := 'July';
      8 : Month := 'August';
      9 : Month := 'September';
     10 : Month := 'October';
     11 : Month := 'November';
     12 : Month := 'December'
   END; {Case}
  END; {With}
  Date := Month +' ' + Day +', ' + Year;
END; {Date}
```

Figure 1.1: (continued)

```
FUNCTION Time : UniversalString;
TYPE
  RegPack = RECORD
      AX, BX, CX, DX, BP, SI, DS, ES, Flags : INTEGER;
    END;
VAR
  Regs: Regpack;
  Test, Dummy : INTEGER;
  Hour, Min, Sec : STRING [2];
BEGIN
   WITH Regs DO
   BEGIN
      AX := $2C00;
      MSDOS (Regs);
      STR (HI (CX), Hour);
      STR (LO (CX), Min);
      STR (HI (DX), Sec)
   END;
   VAL (Min, Test, Dummy);      {This merely allows neater printing
                                 of single-digit values.}
   IF (Test < 10) THEN  Min := '0'+ Min;
   VAL (Sec, Test, Dummy);
   IF (Test < 10) THEN  Sec := '0' + Sec;
   Time := Hour + ':' + Min + ':' + Sec
END;

PROCEDURE WaitForAnyKey;          {Pauses and waits for any key}
VAR
  AnyKey : CHAR;
BEGIN
  WRITELN ('To continue, please strike any key.');
  READ (KBD, AnyKey)
END;

FUNCTION YesOrNo (PromptMessage : UniversalString) : BOOLEAN;

{This function accepts a prompting message from the calling
 program and then accepts both upper- and lowercase responses.
 If the answer is in the affirmative, a Boolean TRUE is returned.
 Note that the string PromptMessage is not a local variable, but
 must be declared for the entire program.}

VAR
  Response : CHAR;

BEGIN
  WRITE(PromptMessage,' (Y/N) ');
  REPEAT
    READ (KBD, Response);
  UNTIL Response IN ['Y','y','N','n'];
  WRITE (Response);
  YesOrNo := Response IN ['Y','y']
END;
```

Figure 1.1: (continued)

```
PROGRAM BasicLibraryRoutines;
{Routines include:
   Beep         to sound beeper.
   Play         to sound any tone for any duration.
   Canada       to play short tune.
   UpString     to convert a string to all upper-case.
   Inc          to increment any integer by one.
   Dec          to decrease any integer by one.
   Dup          to copy any character any number of times.
   Left         to flush string left within a field.
   Right        to flush string right in a field.
   Center       to center a string in a field.
   Power        to raise a real number to an integer power.
   Date         to fetch and decode the date from the operating system.
   Time         to fetch and decode the time from the operating system.
   WaitForKey   to display message and await any user response.
   YesOrNo      to prompt user for Y/N response and pass Boolean
                value back.
}
{$I Routine.inc}

PROCEDURE TestIncrementAndDecrement;  {This will test the Inc and
                                       Dec functions.}
VAR
  TestValue : INTEGER;

BEGIN
  TestValue := 73;
  WRITELN ('The original number is ', TestValue);
  Inc (TestValue);
  WRITELN ('The incremented number is ', TestValue);
  Dec (TestValue);
  WRITELN ('The decremented number is ', TestValue)
END;

PROCEDURE TestWaitForAnyKey;
BEGIN
  WaitForAnyKey;
END;

PROCEDURE TestPrompter;
BEGIN
  IF YesOrNo ('Do you like this prompting message? ') THEN
  BEGIN
    WRITELN;
    WRITELN ('THAT IS GOOD');
    WRITELN
  END
ELSE

  BEGIN
    WRITELN;
    WRITELN ('But at least the YesOrNo function works');
    WRITELN
  END;
END; {TestPrompter}
```

Figure 1.2: The driver program ROUTINE.PAS, which uses and demonstrates the operation of the include file called ROUTINE.INC.

```
PROCEDURE TestUpString;
BEGIN
  WRITELN;
  WRITELN (UpString ('this started out as a lowercase string'));
  WRITELN
END;


PROCEDURE TestDup;
BEGIN
  WRITELN (Dup (80,#2));  {I want a line of 80 smiling faces.}
END;


PROCEDURE TestPlacement;
VAR
  Words : UniversalString;
BEGIN
  Words := 'TURBO LIBRARY TO THE RIGHT IN 60 SPACES';
  WRITELN (Right (Words, 60));
  Words := 'TURBO LIBRARY TO THE LEFT';
  WRITELN (Left (Words, 80));
  Words := 'TURBO LIBRARY CENTERED ON 60 SPACES';
  WRITELN (Center (Words, 60))

END;


PROCEDURE TestPower;
BEGIN
  WRITELN;
  WRITELN ('Five to the second power is: ', Power (5,2));
  WRITELN
END;


PROCEDURE TestDate;
BEGIN
  WRITELN ('Today is: ', Date);
  WRITELN
END;


PROCEDURE TestCanada;
BEGIN
  WRITELN;
  Canada;
  WRITELN
END;


PROCEDURE TestTime;
BEGIN
  WRITELN;
  WRITELN ('The current time is: ', Time);
  WRITELN
END;
```

Figure 1.2: (continued)

```
BEGIN {Main}
  TestDate;
  TestIncrementAndDecrement;
  TestUpString;
  TestPlacement;
  TestTime;
  TestPower;
  WRITELN ('This program tests several routines to make programs
           more readable');
  WRITELN ('Some of the routines simply save some repetitious
           coding,');
  WRITELN ('While others allow procedures with intuitively
           obvious names ');
  WRITELN ('To do some little, repetetive tasks.');
  TestCanada;
  TestWaitForAnyKey;
  TestPrompter;
  TestDup;
  WRITELN ('Obviously, these routines lend themselves to large
           programs,');
  WRITELN ('In which they also help to save lines of code again
           and again.');
  Beep
END.
```

Figure 1.2: (continued)

Bells and Whistles— TITLE.INC, MARCH.PAS, and WINDOWS.INC

The last two include files, *TITLE.INC* and *WINDOWS.INC*, are quite a bit more ambitious than the earlier routines. *TITLE.INC*, listed in Figure 1.3, is used to create large-character titles to fill the screen when program operation is initiated. Such titles can add a professional look to even the simplest program. The operation of the routine appears a bit intimidating at first, primarily because of the convoluted calculations it takes to place the characters where you want them. To make the process of decoding and printing characters clearer, the program in Figure 1.4, *MARCH.PAS*, uses the same character-formation logic, but simply paints a row of up to eight characters "marching" across the screen.

The routine used here is a particularly clever bit of programming (and is not an original idea from the author). Variations of the concept have appeared in dozens of places and have been written in just about every popular programming language. In fact, even among Timex and Sinclair ZX users, a BASIC language version of this was among the most widely distributed programs both here and in the United Kingdom.

In brief, the program creates an array of the bytes of PC memory that contain the patterns the PC monitor uses to create the screen characters. The PC stores each displayable character in eight consecutive bytes of ROM memory. Each bit represents one screen dot (or one pin on a dot-matrix printer), forming an 8 × 8 matrix of dots. Thus, the ones and zeros of each byte correspond directly to the dots turned on or off in one horizontal "slice" of a character. A little research tells us that the location of these patterns (or bit maps) begins at a specific location that will never vary (after all, ROM, by definition, is unalterable). *Table* is the array of these patterns for all displayable characters. Its declaration uses the rarely-seen reserved word ABSOLUTE to begin the array at the starting point in ROM of the character shape table ($F000:$FA6E). Note that this address is specific to the IBM PC; it may need to be changed for some compatibles.

Fortunately for us, the individual bit maps have been stored in ROM in the exact order of the corresponding ASCII codes. This means that the ASCII code for a character is also the index to its unique bit map. Thus the pattern of dots used by your monitor to display an A (ASCII 65) is the 65th item in the array called *Table*.

The procedure *PaintBigCharacter* takes each byte (there are eight altogether) of the bit map and paints a large box for each dot that is turned on in the normal-sized character.

Remember that a dot is represented by a binary one in each byte, and a space by a binary zero. A byte is examined and, by a series of divisions by two, each corresponding bit is tested to see if it is a 1, which should generate a large block, or a 0, which should generate a space instead. The program uses Turbo's windowing techniques to provide a framework for painting each large character.

Division by two is a programming technique that effectively shifts the bits in the byte to allow each to be examined, one at a time. Don't be too concerned if what is happening is not immediately obvious. Even without understanding the actual bit-by-bit analysis of the ROM-resident bit maps, you can still use the procedure to print large characters. Run the *MARCH* program and then look closely at the character shapes that your monitor uses in normal size. You will see that they are the same ones that are enlarged in the *MARCH* program.

All that *TITLE.INC* adds to the *PaintBigCharacter* routine is some valuable—but obscure—control of where the large characters are painted on the screen in a series of windows. To invoke the program, simply call the *PrintMessage* procedure and pass it the text of each line and the starting point (counting down from the top of the screen) of the top of each line of the message. For example:

```
PrintMessage ('UNIVERSAL',1);
PrintMessage ('CONVERSION',9);
PrintMessage ('PROGRAM',17);
```

You will see this routine used frequently throughout the book in conjunction with control over the screen color (using the standard Turbo procedures TEXTCOLOR and TEXTBACKGROUND) and the *WaitForAnyKey* procedure so that the message is not immediately erased as soon as it is displayed.

Creating Windows

The program in Figure 1.5, called *WINDOWS.INC*, is another somewhat complex collection of routines that allow you not only to create different screen windows but to draw attractive borders around them as well. The routines here are the distillation of variations written by many different programmers, gathered from many sources. The key to the operation is to establish a group of limits—the starting and ending points of the window (always the upper-left and lower-right corner points) and to pass these values to a routine that either invokes the standard Turbo WINDOW procedure or plots a user-determined or default pattern of characters to form a frame outside of the window.

In the routines here, the window limits are stored in a data type called, aptly enough, *Corners*. *DoWindow* simply passes these corner values to the Turbo WINDOW procedure.

MakeFrame is a bit more complex; it has to calculate the height and width of the window before it can print a series of horizontal and vertical frame characters as well as the appropriate corner characters. The ASCII character table in your computer reference manual should make the program's operation clearer, as will the ASCII table option in Sidekick. If you don't have those references at hand, remember that the following characters are used by the program:

218 and 201 are the upper-left corner symbols ┌ and ╔
191 and 187 are the upper-right corner symbols ┐ and ╗
192 and 200 are the lower-left corner symbols └ and ╚
217 and 188 are the lower-right corner symbols ┘ and ╝
196 and 205 are the horizontal-line symbols ─ and ═
179 and 186 are the vertical-line symbols │ and ║

Notice that one set is a single line wide, while the second value is for double-line characters.

To use *MakeFrame*, you must pass it a series of parameters:

```
MakeFrame (MetricWindow,#205, #186);
```

In this case *MetricWindow* was a set of corner coordinates defined earlier in the calling program:

```
CONST
    MetricWindow : Corners = (4,8,19,13);
```

The characters #205 and #186 are the horizontal and vertical double-line characters which automatically access the correct (double) corner characters, thanks to the CASE statement in *MakeFrame*. The user has the option of skipping the use of all these rule and corner characters and passing any characters to the procedure. Thus, to get the example *MetricWindow* framed in dollar signs rather than a ruled border, you would type:

```
MakeFrame (MetricWindow, $, $)
```

Again, if the operation of these routines is still unclear, just study the way they are used in the later programs in this book. Even if you don't fully understand their operation, they can be considered as "black boxes" that can be invoked whenever you need them.

```
TYPE
  BitMap = ARRAY[1..8] OF BYTE;
  StringOf11 = STRING [11];
VAR
  Table : ARRAY [0..255] OF BitMap ABSOLUTE $F000:$FA6E;
  Response : StringOf11;
  Row : BYTE;

PROCEDURE PaintBigCharacter  (Entry : BitMap);
VAR
  OnePatternLine, Spot     : 1..8;
  CurrentLine       : BYTE;
BEGIN                                { This procedure is meant to }
  CLRSCR;                            { write into the upper left  }
  FOR OnePatternLine := 1 TO 8 DO    { corner of a window.}
  BEGIN
    CurrentLine := Entry [OnePatternLine];
    {Decodes information one line at a time, from top to bottom.}
    FOR Spot := 8 DOWNTO 1 DO
      BEGIN
        IF ODD (CurrentLine) {If you should output a spot here...}
        THEN
        BEGIN
          GOTOXY (Spot, OnePatternLine);
          WRITE (#178);
          {Use #177 and #176 for dimmer characters, #1 for
           characters made up of smiling faces, and #219 for
           chunkier characters.  Of course, part of the fun is
           using funky characters as well.}
        END;
        CurrentLine := CurrentLine DIV 2;
        {We could also use a shift right.  Now, test the next bit.}
    END;  {Bit number}
  END;   {OnePatternLine}
END;    {Paint Big Character}

PROCEDURE PrintMessage (Message : StringOf11; StartRow : BYTE);
VAR
  N, Lenth, StartColumn, ThisColumn : BYTE;
BEGIN
  Lenth := LENGTH (Message);

  StartColumn := ((80 - 8 * Lenth) DIV 2) AND $00FF;
  FOR N := 1 TO Lenth DO
    BEGIN
      ThisColumn := StartColumn + 8 * (N-1) +1;
      WINDOW (ThisColumn, StartRow, ThisColumn + 7, StartRow + 8);
      PaintBigCharacter (Table[ORD(Message[N])])
    END;
  WINDOW(1,1,80,25);
END; {Print Message}
```

Figure 1.3: The include file TITLE.INC to print large characters on the screen.

```
PROGRAM MarchingDisplay;
TYPE
  BitMap = ARRAY[1..8] OF BYTE;
  {This array holds the complete pattern for one screen
   character's dot matrix, consisting of eight rows of eight
   dots.}

Words = STRING [11];

VAR
  Table : ARRAY [0..255] OF BitMap ABSOLUTE $F000:$FA6E;
  Response : Words;
  Ch : CHAR;
  Row : BYTE;

  {This table contains the bit maps for the complete set of 256
   characters.  It also means that the first element of the array
   is at the stated absolute address, which just happens to be
   where the IBM PC stores its character shapes in its reserved
   parts of memory.}

PROCEDURE PaintBigCharacter   (Entry : BitMap);
VAR
  OnePatternLine, Spot     : 1..8;
  CurrentLine       : BYTE;
BEGIN                                 { This procedure is meant to }
  CLRSCR;                             { write into the upper left  }
    FOR OnePatternLine := 1 TO 8 DO   { corner of a window. }
      BEGIN
        CurrentLine := Entry [OnePatternLine];
        {Decodes information one line at a time, from top to
         bottom.}
        FOR Spot := 8 DOWNTO 1 DO
          BEGIN
            IF ODD (CurrentLine) {If you should output a spot here...}
            THEN
            BEGIN
              GOTOXY (Spot, OnePatternLine);
              WRITE (#178);
              {Use #177 and #176 for dimmer characters, #1 for
               characters made up of smiling faces, and #219 for
               chunkier characters.  Of course part of the fun is
               using funky characters as well.}
            END;
          CurrentLine := CurrentLine DIV 2;
          {We could also use a shift right.  Now, test the next bit.}
        END; {Bit}
    END; {OnePatternLine}
END;     {PaintBigCharacter}

PROCEDURE PrintMessage (Message : Words; Starting_row : BYTE);
VAR
  N, lenth, starting_col, this_col : BYTE;
BEGIN
  lenth := LENGTH(Message);
```

Figure 1.4: The program MARCH.PAS to demonstrate the creation of large character images, but without any automatic procedure for automatically centering the message lines on the screen.

```
    starting_col := ((80 - 8*lenth) DIV 2) AND $00FF;
    FOR N := 1 TO lenth DO
      BEGIN
        this_col := starting_col + 8*(N-1) +1;
        WINDOW(this_col,starting_row,this_col+7,starting_row+8);
        PaintBigCharacter(table[ORD(Message[N])])
      END;
    WINDOW(1,1,80,25)
  END;


  PROCEDURE Title (ASCIISymbol : CHAR; Col, Row : BYTE);
  BEGIN
     WINDOW (col, row, col+7, row+8);
     PaintBigCharacter (Table [ORD (ASCIISymbol)]);
     WINDOW (1,1,80,25)
  END;



  PROCEDURE TryItOut;
  VAR
    Count : INTEGER;
    Cl, Next, Third, Fourth  : CHAR;
  BEGIN
    CLRSCR;
    WRITELN ('Type a character');
    Count := 72;
    REPEAT
      READ (KBD, Cl);
      Title (Cl, Count ,8);
      Count := Count - 8; {Move over the width of one character.}
      IF Count = 0 THEN Count := 72;
      READ (KBD, Next);
      CLRSCR;
      Title (Cl, Count, 8);
      Title (Next, Count+8, 8);
      Count := Count - 8; {Move over the width of one character.}
      READ (KBD, Third);
      CLRSCR;
      Title (Cl, Count, 8);
      Title (Next, Count+8, 8) ;
      Title (Third, Count+16, 8) ;
      Count := Count - 8; {Move over the width of one character.}
      READ (KBD, Fourth);
      CLRSCR;
      Title (Cl, Count, 8);
      Title (Next, Count+8, 8)   ;
      Title (Third, Count+16, 8)   ;
      Title (Fourth, Count+24, 8)    ;
      Count := Count - 8; {Move over the width of one character.}
    UNTIL (Cl = '.')
  END;
```

Figure 1.4: (continued)

```
BEGIN
  Row := 5;
  CLRSCR;
  WRITELN ('What do you have to say?');
  Response :='';
  CLRSCR;
  REPEAT
    READ (KBD, Ch);
    Response := Response + Ch;
    IF (Ch = #13) THEN
    BEGIN
      ROW := 14;
      Response := ''
    END;
  PrintMessage (Response, Row);
  UNTIL (Ch = '.')
END.
```

Figure 1.4: (continued)

```
TYPE
  Corners = ARRAY[1..4] OF BYTE;

PROCEDURE DoWindow (OneCorner : Corners);
BEGIN
  WINDOW (OneCorner[1], OneCorner[2], OneCorner[3], OneCorner[4]);
  GOTOXY (1,1)
END;

PROCEDURE MakeFrame (OneCorner : Corners ; Horiz, Vertical : CHAR);
VAR
  FrameCorners : ARRAY[1..4] OF CHAR;
  Index        : BYTE;
BEGIN
  WINDOW (1,1,80,25);
  CASE Horiz OF
    #196 : BEGIN
             FrameCorners[1] := #218;
             FrameCorners[2] := #191;
             FrameCorners[3] := #192;
             FrameCorners[4] := #217
           END;
    #205: BEGIN
             FrameCorners[1] := #201;
             FrameCorners[2] := #187;
             FrameCorners[3] := #200;
             FrameCorners[4] := #188
          END;
    ELSE
      FOR Index := 1 TO 4 DO
        FrameCorners[Index] := Horiz;
  END;  {Case}
  GOTOXY (OneCorner[1]-1, OneCorner[2]-1);
  WRITE (FrameCorners[1]);
  FOR Index := OneCorner[1] TO OneCorner[3] DO WRITE (Horiz);
  WRITE (FrameCorners[2]);
  FOR Index := OneCorner[2] TO OneCorner[4] DO
    BEGIN
      GOTOXY (OneCorner[3]+1, Index);
      WRITE (Vertical)
    END;
  GOTOXY (OneCorner[3]+1, OneCorner[4]+1);
  WRITE (FrameCorners[4]);
  FOR Index := OneCorner[3] DOWNTO OneCorner[1] DO
    BEGIN
      GOTOXY (Index,OneCorner[4]+1);
      WRITE (Horiz)
    END;
  GOTOXY (OneCorner[1]-1, OneCorner[4]+1); WRITE (FrameCorners[3]);
  FOR Index := OneCorner[4] DOWNTO OneCorner[2] DO

    BEGIN
      GOTOXY (OneCorner[1]-1, Index);
      WRITE (Vertical)
    END
END; {MakeFrame}
```

Figure 1.5: The include file WINDOWS.INC both creates screen windows and frames them automatically.

2 Manipulating Data Structures

Introduction

The programs in this chapter involve the manipulation of data structures. A few programs deal specifically with text files—getting a directory, checking for file-processing errors, and altering the contents of the files. Other programs—like the timer and sorting routines—lend themselves to applications involving arrays, pointers, and lists. Because so many programs deal with data structures, you are sure to find several techniques and routines in this chapter that you can apply to projects today.

Displaying a DOS Directory—DIRECTRY.PAS

Figure 2.1 is a listing of the program *DIRECTRY.PAS*, which generates and displays a DOS directory. It accepts the usual DOS wildcard characters. Versions of this program available on different bulletin boards will display the directory in alphabetical order, by size, or by date and will give a complete readout of the size and file attributes of each file. Sources listed in the Appendix, along with the Turbo manual, would contain information on modifying this program for the CP/M operating system.

The version shown here gives a simple, straightforward list of the files in the current directory. The operating system does all the real work in this program, through powerful BDOS functions. Thus, to understand exactly what is going on, you need to be familiar with the information in the technical reference guide for DOS. The Appendix lists alternative sources for this information, as well.

In many ways, this program works much like the *Date* and *Time* routines from the first chapter. Specific values are loaded into system registers, and an operating-system function is invoked. The operating system places values into these registers, and Turbo in turn reads these registers and displays the information contained there. If you have even a basic understanding of DOS, the variable names and comments included with the code in Figure 2.1 should explain in more detail the operation of the routine and what information is stored where.

Again, although it takes a thorough knowledge of the operating system, register usage, BDOS and BIOS calls, and system interrupts to *modify* routines like this, you can still *use* them just as if they were standard Turbo procedures. And, of course, you can experiment with them—particularly in the "safer" areas (not dealing with the operating system) of formatting the data output.

```
PROGRAM Directory;
  {Versions of this program appear on just about every bulletin
   board.}

PROCEDURE Directry;
TYPE
  ArrayToHoldMask              = ARRAY [1..14] OF CHAR;
  StringToHoldFileName         = STRING [20];
  RegRecord =
    RECORD
      AX, BX, CX, DX, BP, SI, DI, DS, ES, Flags : INTEGER;
    END
VAR
  RegisterContents   : RegRecord;
  DTA                : ARRAY [1..43] OF BYTE;
    {DTA stands for Disk Transfer Area and is the area used by
     DOS to buffer the information it returns concerning directory
     information.}
  Mask               : ArrayToHoldMask;
  FileName           : StringToHoldFileName;
  Error, I           : INTEGER;

PROCEDURE SetUpDOS;
BEGIN
  FILLCHAR (DTA, 43, 0);      {These lines initialize everything.}
  FILLCHAR (Mask, 14, 0);
  FILLCHAR (FileName, 20, 0);
  WRITELN;
    {These next three lines give DOS a place to put the raw
     directory information.}
  RegisterContents.AX := $1A00;
  RegisterContents.DS := SEG (DTA);
  RegisterContents.DX := OFS (DTA);
   {The next line merely passes the setup information to DOS}
  MSDOS (RegisterContents);
  Error := 0
END;

PROCEDURE DecodeDirectoryEntry;
  {Converts the information returned by DOS into
   neat, screen-printable entries without all the file attribute
   information.}
BEGIN
  REPEAT
    FileName [I] := CHR (MEM [SEG (DTA) : OFS (DTA) + 29 + I]);
    I := I + 1;
  UNTIL NOT (FileName [I-1] IN [' '..' ']) OR (I>20);
  FileName [0] := CHR (I-1);
END

PROCEDURE DetermineMask;
BEGIN
  WRITELN ('What Mask should I use?');
  READLN (Mask);
END;
```

Figure 2.1: The program DIRECTRY.PAS to read a DOS directory. The program supports wildcard entries.

```
PROCEDURE CallDOS;
BEGIN
  RegisterContents.DS := SEG (Mask);    { Point to the Mask file.}
  RegisterContents.DX := OFS (Mask);
  RegisterContents.CX := 22;
  MSDOS (RegisterContents);               { Execute MSDOS call }
  Error := RegisterContents.AX AND $FF;  { DOS says there are no
                                            files that match the
                                            mask. }
  I := 1;
  SetUpDOS;
  DetermineMask;
  RegisterContents.AX := $4E00;         { Get FIRST directory entry }
  CallDOS;
  IF (Error = 0) THEN
    WHILE (Error = 0) DO
    BEGIN DecodeDirectoryEntry;
      Error := 0;
      RegisterContents.AX := $4F00;          { Get NEXT directory entry}
      CallDOS;
      DecodeDirectoryEntry;
      IF (Error = 0)
      THEN WRITELN (FileName)
    END; {WHILE}
END; {CallDOS}

PROCEDURE TestDirectory;
BEGIN
  Directry;
END;

BEGIN
  TestDirectory;
END.
```

Figure 2.1: (continued)

Deleting Files from within Turbo—DELFILE.PAS

Figure 2.2 contains a program, called *DELFILE.PAS,* that allows you to delete files without leaving the Turbo environment to use the operating system's file-erasure command. It is most useful not as a stand-alone program but when the *Delete* procedure is integrated into a larger program. With files manipulating important data (sorting, alphabetizing, filtering, and so forth), I prefer to use separate input and output file names rather than have the routine automatically overwrite the source file name. When the files have been processed correctly, a program user can be queried and his response used as input to the *Delete* routine. Thus, the *Delete* procedure is a handy way for the user to do his file-management housekeeping.

The procedure *TestDelete* simply exercises the *Delete* routine, which does all the nitty-gritty file assignments before invoking the Turbo ERASE procedure.

```
PROGRAM DeleteFile;
{$I-}   {Turns off Turbo's error checking}


PROCEDURE Delete;
TYPE
  FileName = STRING[14] ;
VAR
  NameOfFileToBeDeleted     : FileName ;
  TemporaryNameForFile  : FILE ;
BEGIN
  WRITELN ;
  WRITELN ('This procedure deletes a file from within the Turbo
           environment.') ;
  WRITELN ('Changed your mind?  Just hit Return and nothing is
           gone.')  ;
  WRITELN ;
  WRITE    ('Name of file to delete? (can include drive
             specifier) ');
  READLN  (NameOfFileToBeDeleted) ;
  IF NameOfFileToBeDeleted <> '' THEN
    BEGIN
      ASSIGN  (TemporaryNameForFile, NameOfFileToBeDeleted) ;
      ERASE    (TemporaryNameForFile) ;
      IF IORESULT = 0 THEN
        WRITELN ('File ', NameOfFileToBeDeleted, ' successfully deleted')
      ELSE
        WRITELN ('I cannot find a file with that name.')
    END;
END; {Delete}

PROCEDURE TestDelete;
VAR
  TestFile : TEXT;
BEGIN
  CLRSCR;
  ASSIGN (TestFile, 'DEADDUCK.XXX');
  REWRITE (TestFile);
  WRITE (TestFile, #07);
  CLOSE (TestFile);
  WRITELN ('File DEADDUCK.XXX successfully created.');
  Delete;
END;

BEGIN
  TestDelete
END.
```

Figure 2.2: The program DELFILE.PAS to delete a file from within the Turbo environment. You can incorporate a version of this program into a larger program or use it as it is.

Trapping Errors— IOERR.PAS

The program *IOERR.PAS* in Figure 2.3 is more an illustration of a concept than a universally useful program. It simply interrupts the Turbo error handler and prints out an informative error message rather than the cryptic Borland error codes. It is a simple application of a CASE structure to print out the correct error message based on the specific error code returned by Turbo's IORESULT function.

Frankly, it is a bit cumbersome to sprinkle calls to the *IOCheck* procedure throughout a program. I have found this procedure most useful during program development, at those times when I cannot easily locate the exact part of a routine causing the usual Turbo messages. Thus, I only include the procedure and insert the calls to *IOCheck* when my normal debugging efforts don't point to an immediately obvious error.

The concept, however, of a routine to trap errors and do something about them (in this case, simply translating an error code into a human-readable message) can be applied to many user-oriented programs. The routine can be made even more useful in end-user programs if you don't just print an error message, but also print out a suggested remedial action.

```
{$I-,R-}
PROGRAM DecipherErrorNumbers;

PROCEDURE WaitForAnyKey;        {Copied here from our standard library.}
VAR
  AnyKey : CHAR;
BEGIN
  WRITELN;       {The prompts can be put in the calling program instead.}
  WRITELN ('To continue, please strike any key.');
  READ (KBD, AnyKey);
  WRITELN;
END;

PROCEDURE Play (Note, Time : INTEGER);
 {Used like Beep and also to play real tunes, this procedure
  gives control over both pitch and duration of sound.}
BEGIN
  SOUND (Note);
  DELAY (Time);
  NOSOUND
END;

PROCEDURE IOCheck;
CONST
  CrypticMessageNumber : INTEGER = 0;       {Initialized to zero}
  ErrorFlag              : BOOLEAN = FALSE; {Initialized to false}
BEGIN
  CrypticMessageNumber := IORESULT;
  ErrorFlag := (CrypticMessageNumber <> 0);
      {Set error flag if and only if the IORESULT function
       returns a value other than zero.}
  IF ErrorFlag THEN BEGIN
    PLAY (440, 600);
    CASE CrypticMessageNumber OF
      $01  :  WRITE('File does not exist');
      $02  :  WRITE('File not open for input');
      $03  :  WRITE('File not open for output');
      $04  :  WRITE('File not open');
      $05  :  WRITE('Can''t read from this file');
      $06  :  WRITE('Can''t write to this file');
      $10  :  WRITE('Error in numeric format');
      $20  :  WRITE('Operation not allowed on a logical device');
      $21  :  WRITE('Not allowed in direct mode');
      $22  :  WRITE('Assign to standard files not allowed');
      $90  :  WRITE('Record length mismatch');
      $91  :  WRITE('Seek beyond end of file');
      $99  :  WRITE('Unexpected end of file');
      $F0  :  WRITE('Disk write error');
      $F1  :  WRITE('Directory is full');
      $F2  :  WRITE('File size overflow');
      $FF  :  WRITE('File disappeared')
```

Figure 2.3: The program IOERR.PAS to interpret Turbo's I/O errors during program development. The elements shown in this program would not be included in a finished program.

```
    ELSE      WRITE('Unknown I/O error:  ',CrypticMessageNumber:3)
    END; {Case}
    WaitForAnyKey
  END {If}
END; {IOcheck}

PROCEDURE TestError;  {Tests procedure}
VAR
  InFile     : TEXT;
  Line       : STRING[80];
BEGIN
  ASSIGN (InFile,'XXXX');
  IOCheck;
  RESET (InFile);
  IOCheck;
  READ (Infile, Line);
  IOCheck;
  CLOSE (Infile);
  IOCheck
END;

BEGIN
  TestError
END.
```

Figure 2.3: (continued)

Filtering a Text File— FILTER.PAS

One of the more useful routines that I have had to develop myself is shown in Figure 2.4. This is a simple filter to read a text file and quite literally filter out any character found between the European quote marks (<< and >>). In converting the output of my XyWrite word-processor into the input to a typesetting system, I had to filter out all the XyWrite formatting and control codes that were embedded in the text file. The *FILTER.PAS* program was a fast, simple, way to remove any characters bracketed by the XyWrite command delimiters—the European quotes.

The program offers two unusual features. Because XyWrite supports nested commands, a simple toggle ("stop output until you see the end-command character") would not work when I had chosen to use these sophisticated commands within command sequences. Thus, a counter (*PassCharThru*) is used to ensure that output is not resumed until the filter has processed an end-command delimiter for every begin-command delimiter.

The second interesting feature of this filter program is that it automatically takes the filtered file and gives it the name of the input file. In a neatly polished program, this technique prevents the user from seeing the intermediate or scratch files used by many sorting and filtering programs. This technique is both powerful and dangerous! As a bit of cheap insurance, then, I first rename the input file as *ORIGINAL.BAK* before renaming the filtered file with the original file name.

```
PROGRAM FilterFileWhileRetainingOriginalFileName;
{$I ROUTINE.INC}

VAR
  OneChar: CHAR;
  InFile, OutFile: TEXT;
  PassCharThru: INTEGER;
  InputFileName : STRING[14];

PROCEDURE Initialize;
BEGIN
  CLRSCR;
  ScreenMessage ('What is the input file?');
  READLN (InputFileName);
  ASSIGN (InFile, InputFileName);
  ASSIGN (OutFile, '$$$.$$$');  {Temporary file name}
  RESET (InFile);
  REWRITE (OutFile);
  PassCharThru:=0
END;

PROCEDURE Stripper;
BEGIN
  WHILE NOT EOF(Infile) DO
  BEGIN
    READ (Infile, OneChar);
    IF OneChar = #174 THEN PassCharThru := PassCharThru + 1
    IF OneChar = #175 THEN
      BEGIN
        PassCharThru := PassCharThru-1;
        READ (Infile,OneChar);
        IF OneChar = #174 THEN PassCharThru := PassCharThru+1;
      END;
    IF PassCharThru = 0 THEN
      BEGIN
        WRITE (OutFile,OneChar);
        WRITE (OneChar)  {echo action to screen for debugging}
      END
  END {While}
END; {Stripper}

PROCEDURE UpdateOriginalFileName;
BEGIN
  RENAME (InFile, 'ORIGINAL.BAK');    {Cheap insurance for faint-
                                        hearted programmers}
  RENAME (OutFile, InputFileName)
END;
```

Figure 2.4: The program FILTER.PAS is an example of a program to open a text file and process its contents. In this case it removes the commands embedded in a text file by the XyWrite word processor. One feature of the program is that the processed file retains the same name as the unprocessed file.

```
BEGIN
  Initialize;
  Stripper;
  CLOSE (Infile);
  CLOSE (Outfile);
  UpdateOriginalFileName;
  Beep
  WRITELN ('File  ', InputFileName, ' has been processed successfully')
END.
```

Figure 2.4: (continued)

A Variation on the FILTER.PAS Program

In Figure 2.5 there is a simple variation on the *Stripper* routine used by *FILTER.PAS*. This, too, was written in response to a real, ad hoc need. I received a group of programs written by the user of a VT-100 terminal. Although the programs compiled very nicely under my copy of Turbo, their listings were hard to read because they were cluttered with the Control-I (tab or ASCII 9) character from the VT-100 display. The modified *Stripper* routine did a great job of cleaning up the listing. Note that the method used here is actually simpler than the routine in Figure 2.4, because there was no need to use a counter. Any occurrence of the Control-I character was simply not written to the output file. This routine illustrates how much easier it is to modify a well-proven program (in this case, *FILTER.PAS*) than to write a complete program from scratch.

```
PROCEDURE Stripper;
BEGIN
  WHILE NOT EOF(Infile) DO
  BEGIN
    READ (Infile, OneChar);
    IF OneChar = #9 THEN  WRITELN
      ELSE
      BEGIN
        WRITE (OutFile,OneChar);
        WRITE (OneChar);  {echo action to screen for debugging}
      END;
  END {While}
END; {Stripper}
```

Figure 2.5: A variation on FILTER.PAS to show the simple modification needed to filter out extraneous tab commands.

Making Certain Words Uppercase—UPCASE.PAS

Figure 2.6 illustrates an ambitious application of text filters. The program *UPCASE.PAS* reads a Turbo source file and puts all the reserved words into uppercase to make your listings more readable. Versions of this program can be found on many bulletin boards, and the basic operation can, of course, be applied to tasks other than producing a program listing. For example, a data file can be processed to put all state abbreviations in uppercase.

Of course, an even more ambitious variation of text filtering would be to actually reformat data—for instance, substituting common street abbreviations (St., Blvd., Rd.) when the words were found spelled out in full.

UPCASE opens a file and parses it line by line, while carefully leaving print strings and comments unaltered. Each line is broken into individual words; each word on the line, in turn, is automatically put into all caps, but the original version of the word is also retained. Each word is compared with a table of constants (*ReservedWords1* through *ReservedWords14*), looking for a match. If the word matches, the uppercase version is printed to the output file. If no match is found, the original version is printed. It is a clever and elegant—if not immediately obvious—routine.

The details of the program operation should be clear from the comments and the informatively named identifiers.

```
PROGRAM UpCase;

{$I routine.inc}
{Based on a bulletin board program by Jeff Firestone}

CONST
  ReservedWords1 = ' ARCTAN ASSIGN AUX AUXINPTR AUXOUTPTR
                   BLOCKREAD BLOCKWRITE BOOLEAN BDOS ';
  ReservedWords2 = ' BUFLEN BYTE CHAIN CHAR CHR CLOSE CLREOL
                   CLRSCR CON CONINPTR HALT BIOS ';
  ReservedWords3 = ' CONCAT CONSTPTR COPY COS CRTEXIT CRTINIT
                   DELLINE DELAY DELETE LOWVIDEO ';
  ReservedWords4 = ' EOF EOLN ERASE EXECUTE EXP FALSE FILEPOS
                   FILESIZE FILLCHAR FLUSH INTR ';
  ReservedWords5 = ' FRAC GETMEM GOTOXY HEAPPTR HI HIGHVIDEO
                   IORESULT INPUT INSLINE INSERT ';
  ReservedWords6 = ' INT INTEGER KBD KEYPRESSED LENGTH LN LO LST
                   LSTOUTPTR MARK MAXINT MEM ';
  ReservedWords7 = ' MEMAVAIL MOVE NEW NORMVIDEO ODD ORD OUTPUT
                   PI PORT POS PRED PTR RANDOM ';
  ReservedWords8 = ' RANDOMIZE READ READLN REAL RELEASE RENAME
                   RESET REWRITE ROUND SEEK SIN ';
  ReservedWords9 = ' SIZEOF SQR SQRT STR SUCC SWAP TEXT TRM TRUE
                   TRUNC UPCASE USR USRINPTR';
  ReservedWords10= ' USROUTPTR VAL WRITE WRITELN ABSOLUTE AND
                   ARRAY BEGIN CASE CONST DIV ADDR ';
  ReservedWords11= ' DO DOWNTO ELSE END EXTERNAL FILE FOR FORWARD
                   FUNCTION GOTO IF IN COLOR ';
  ReservedWords12= ' INLINE LABEL MOD NIL NOT OF OR PACKED
                   PROCEDURE PROGRAM RECORD REPEAT';
  ReservedWords13= ' SET SHL SHR STRING THEN TO TYPE UNTIL VAR
                   WHILE WITH XOR OFS SEG MEM MEMW ';
  ReservedWords14= ' OVERLAY DISPOSE DRAW FREEMEM HIRES PALLETTE
                   PLOT SOUND WINDOW MAXAVAIL ';

  PrintStringDelimiter = #39;    { This is the ' symbol.}
  OpenComment          = '{';
  CloseComment         = '}';
  OpenParen            = '(';
  CloseParen           = ')';
  Null                 = '';
TYPE
  Caps = SET OF 'A'..'Z';
  Nums = SET OF '0'..'9';
VAR
  CharacterPosition, LineNum  : INTEGER;
  ProgramLine, FileName, TmpWord, TmpWrd : UniversalString;
     {Remember that UniversalString is defined in the include file.}
  RawWord                     : STRING [100];
  InputFile, OutputFile       : TEXT;
  Identifier                  : SET OF CHAR;

PROCEDURE OpenFiles;
BEGIN
  WRITE ('What is the name of the source code file (RETURN to
         end) : ');
```

Figure 2.6: The program UPCASE.PAS to read a Turbo source program and put all reserved words into uppercase letters. This is just a very ambitious form of text-file filter.

```
  READLN (FileName);
  IF LENGTH (FileName) = 0 THEN HALT;
  IF (POS ('.', FileName) = 0) THEN FileName:= FileName + '.PAS';
  ASSIGN (InputFile, FileName);
  RESET (InputFile);
  WRITE ('Where do you want the output to be sent (RETURN for
        Screen) : ');
  READLN (FileName);
  FileName :=  UpString (FileName);
  IF LENGTH (FileName) = 0 THEN FileName:= 'CON:';
  (* Useful technique to direct output to screen. *)
  ASSIGN (OutputFile, FileName);
  REWRITE (OutputFile);
  CLRSCR;
  WRITELN
END; {OpenFiles}

PROCEDURE TestForReservedWords;
VAR
 ReservedWordFlag : INTEGER;
BEGIN
  TmpWrd := UpString (RawWord);
  TmpWord:= ' ' + TmpWrd + ' ';
  { In the following code you really don't care what the
   position number is; all you care about is that a number other
   than zero is returned. }

  ReservedWordFlag:= POS(TmpWord, ReservedWords1) + POS(TmpWord,
                ReservedWords2) +
              POS(TmpWord, ReservedWords3) + POS(TmpWord,
                ReservedWords4) +
              POS(TmpWord, ReservedWords5) + POS(TmpWord,
                ReservedWords6) +
              POS(TmpWord, ReservedWords7) + POS(TmpWord,
                ReservedWords8) +
              POS(TmpWord, ReservedWords9) + POS(TmpWord,
                ReservedWords10) +
              POS(TmpWord, ReservedWords11) + POS(TmpWord,
                ReservedWords12) +
              POS(TmpWord, ReservedWords13) + POS(TmpWord,
                ReservedWords14);
  IF ReservedWordFlag > 0 THEN
    BEGIN
    WRITE (OutputFile, TmpWrd);
{
This is a Debug statement, useful for tracking parser operation.
    WRITELN ('Reserved Word is ',TmpWrd);
 }

    END
  ELSE
    WRITE (OutputFile, RawWord)
END; {TestForReservedWords}

PROCEDURE OutputOneCharacter;
BEGIN
  WRITE (OutputFile, ProgramLine [CharacterPosition])
END;
```

Figure 2.6: (continued)

```
PROCEDURE ProcessAWord;
BEGIN
  RawWord:= '';
  WHILE (UPCASE (ProgramLine [CharacterPosition]) IN Identifier)
    AND
    (CharacterPosition <= LENGTH (ProgramLine)) DO
    BEGIN
      RawWord:= RawWord + ProgramLine [CharacterPosition];
      { To see operation of this parser, un-comment the next line. }
      (*       writeln ('word = ',RawWord); *)
      Inc (CharacterPosition);
    END;
  TestForReservedWords
END; {ProcessAWord}


PROCEDURE ScanTill (SearchChar: CHAR);
BEGIN
  REPEAT
    OutputOneCharacter;
    Inc (CharacterPosition);
    IF CharacterPosition > LENGTH (ProgramLine) THEN
    BEGIN
      WRITELN (OutputFile);  {Simply terminates current line on output.}
      READLN (InputFile, ProgramLine); {Gets the next input line.}
      CharacterPosition:= 1
    END;
  UNTIL (ProgramLine[CharacterPosition] = SearchChar) OR
             EOF(InputFile);
  OutputOneCharacter;
  Inc (CharacterPosition)
END; {ScanTill}


PROCEDURE PassCommentsThroughUnaltered;
{Note that this procedure filters only brace comments, while
 still capitalizing the parenthesis/asterisk comments.}
BEGIN
  ScanTill (CloseComment)
END;


PROCEDURE PassPrintStringThroughUnaltered;
BEGIN
  ScanTill (PrintStringDelimiter)
END;


PROCEDURE Convert;
BEGIN
  LineNum:= 0;
  WHILE NOT EOF(InputFile) DO
  BEGIN
    CharacterPosition:= 1;
    READLN (InputFile, ProgramLine);
    IF LENGTH (ProgramLine) > 0 THEN
    BEGIN
```

Figure 2.6: (continued)

```
    REPEAT
      CASE UPCASE (ProgramLine[CharacterPosition]) OF
           'A'..'Z', '0'..'9', '_'  : ProcessAWord;
           OpenComment              : PassCommentsThroughUnaltered;
           PrintStringDelimiter     : PassPrintStringThroughUnaltered
        ELSE
          BEGIN
            OutputOneCharacter;
            Inc (CharacterPosition)
          END
      END; {Case}
    UNTIL (CharacterPosition > LENGTH (ProgramLine));
    WRITELN (OutputFile);
    IF FileName <> 'CON:' THEN
      BEGIN
        GOTOXY (14, 3);
        WRITE ('Processing line: ', LineNum);
        Inc (LineNum)
      END
    END; {If}
    IF LENGTH (ProgramLine) = 0 THEN WRITELN (OutputFile);
    {This handles blank lines in the source program.}
  END; {While}
  CLOSE (InputFile);
  CLOSE(OutputFile)
END;

BEGIN
  Identifier:= ['A'..'Z', '0'..'9', '_'];
  CLRSCR;
   {Note: These are the only valid characters that can be used in
    Turbo identifiers.}
  OpenFiles;
  Convert
END.
```

Figure 2.6: (continued)

A Timed Shell Sort—TIMESORT.PAS, SELL.INC, and TIMER.INC

In teaching about computers, I find that students are always impressed with the operation of the program shown in Figure 2.7. This is the well-known Shell-Metzner sort, coupled with a routine to calculate and print out the time it takes for the sort to work. The Shell sort is performed by the routines listed separately in Figure 2.8, while the routines used for the time calculation are listed in Figure 2.9.

The program *TIMESORT.PAS* combines the sorting and time routines with a short driver program to test everything. As printed, the routine sorts 100 (*MaxElement*) random numbers, but it is fun to change this number to 250, 500, 1000, 2000, 4000, and 8000 entries and compare the timings. Typical timings for these figures are shown in a comment at the beginning of the listing.

The sort is timed by using a minor variation on the *Time* routine from Chapter 1, which fetches the current time from the operating system including hundredths of seconds. However, there is no need here to convert the information to a string format as we did in the *Time* routine. Instead, it is kept as a real number. The *Timer* routine is called before the sort program, the time is stored as a variable (*Starting*), and the time is fetched again at the end of the sort and stored as a second variable (*Ending*). The difference between the two values is, of course, the time it took to accomplish the sort.

The operation of the sorting routine *Sort,* contained in the include file *SHELL.INC* in Figure 2.8, is described at length in several of the books listed in the Appendix. Briefly, a Shell sort program looks at the total number of elements to be sorted (*MaxElement*) and determines the elements that would be the first element and the element midway through the range (*Gap*). These elements are compared and, if out of order, they are swapped. In a huge group swapping elements in widely different locations *with one operation* can save a great amount of time compared with the simpler bubble sort, which can only move an out-of-place element one position at a time. Once elements separated by the number of positions represented by *Gap* are all compared, *Gap* is halved and the routine is repeated. *Gap* is continually halved until the routine compares adjacent elements.

To get a feel for the operation of the Shell sort, remove the commented line near the end of the listing, and you will see a running screen display of the operation of the program.

The Shell sort is one of the best compromises between program complexity and speed. There are several sorting routines that attempt to calculate how scrambled up the starting group is, in order to compute the optimum *Gap* value and thus further refine the Shell sort, but the version here is quite serviceable for most applications. Although this example sorts a group of random numbers, the sorting logic can be applied to an array of records, a group of pointers, a list of words, or a wide range of other kinds of data and data structures.

```
PROGRAM ShellSortWithElapsedTimeDisplay;
  {Gets time from DOS and computes elapsed time of Shell sort.}
{$I Timer.inc}

{Timings for alternate values of MaxElement are:
 250    0.49
 500    1.15
 1000   2.74
 2000   7.30
 4000   15.43
 8000   39.10
 }

CONST
  MaxElement  = 100;
TYPE
  Target = ARRAY [1..MaxElement] OF INTEGER;
VAR
  Nums  : Target;
  Index : INTEGER;
  BeginSort, EndSort, PrintAndSort : REAL;

{$I Shell.inc}


PROCEDURE Driver;
BEGIN
  CLRSCR;
  WRITELN ('The sort program begins now.');
  WRITELN;
  FOR Index := 1 TO MaxElement DO
      Nums[Index] := RANDOM (5000)
END;

PROCEDURE PrintOut ;     {Prints array contents in ten
                          right-aligned columns.}
BEGIN
  FOR Index := 1 TO MaxElement DO
  BEGIN
  WRITE (Nums[Index]:8);
  END;
  WRITELN;
END;
```

Figure 2.7: The program TIMESORT.PAS to demonstrate both the Shell-sort routine and the Timer function to calculate elapsed time.

```
BEGIN
   Driver;
   WRITELN ('The randomly generated numbers are:');
   PrintOut;
   GetCurrentTime (BeginSort);
   Sort;
   GetCurrentTime (EndSort);
   WRITELN ('The sorted numbers are:');

   PrintOut;
   GetCurrentTime (PrintAndSort);
   WRITE ('It took ', (ElapsedTime (BeginSort, EndSort)):3:2, '
         seconds ');
   WRITELN ('for just the sorting  of ',MaxElement,' numbers.');
   WRITE ('It took ', (ElapsedTime (BeginSort,
         PrintAndSort)):3:2, ' seconds ');
   WRITELN ('for the sorting and printing of ',MaxElement,'
           numbers.')
END.
```

Figure 2.7: (continued)

```
{Shell sort include file}

VAR
 Max, Temp, I, J, Pass, Gap : INTEGER;

PROCEDURE FlipFlop;
BEGIN
  Temp := Nums[J];
  Nums[J] := Nums[J+Gap];
  Nums[J+Gap] := Temp
END;

PROCEDURE Sort;
BEGIN
  Gap := MaxElement DIV 2;
  WHILE Gap > 0 DO
  BEGIN
    FOR I := (Gap + 1) TO MaxElement DO
      BEGIN
        J := I-Gap;
        WHILE J > 0 DO
          IF Nums [J] > Nums [J+Gap] THEN
          BEGIN
            FlipFlop;
            J := J-Gap;
          END
          ELSE J := 0
        END; {While J > 0}
    Gap := Gap DIV 2;
    {For a running display of the shell sort at work, change
     MaxElement to 10, and call the PrinOut procedure here }
  END; {While Gap > 0}
END;
```

Figure 2.8: The file SHELL.INC containing the Shell-sort logic used in the program TIMESORT.PAS.

```
PROCEDURE GetCurrentTime (VAR TotalTimeInHundredths : REAL);
 {Gets time from DOS and converts to a total of hundreds of
  seconds.  Although it is similar to the time-stamp routine
  covered earlier, note that this procedure does not convert the
  numbers returned by DOS into strings, but retains them as real
  numbers to allow further computation.  Thus this procedure
  returns a real value, not a string.}
TYPE
  RegisterRecord = RECORD
      AX, BX, CX, DX, BP, SI, DS, ES, Flags : INTEGER
    END;
VAR
  Regs: RegisterRecord;
  Hours, Mins, Secs, Hundredths : REAL;
BEGIN
  WITH Regs DO
  BEGIN
    AX := $2C00; {Hex 2C gets the time.}
    MsDos (Regs);{We could just as have easily used the INTR function.}
    Hours := HI (CX);
    Mins  := LO (CX);
    Secs := HI (DX);
    Hundredths := LO (DX)
  END;
  TotalTimeInHundredths := ((18000 * Hours) * 2) + (6000 * Mins) +
                 (100 * Secs) + Hundredths;
END; {GetCurrentTime}

FUNCTION ElapsedTime (Starting, Ending : REAL) : REAL;
BEGIN
  ElapsedTime := (Ending - Starting)/100
END;
```

Figure 2.9: The file TIMER.INC containing the modified Time routine from ROUTINE.PAS.

A Binary Search— BINARY.PAS

The program in Figure 2.10 is a personal favorite. It demonstrates the blinding speed of a binary search of *an ordered group*. The key to the program is that the search must take place on an ordered data structure (in numerical or alphabetical order). The version shown in Figure 2.10 is implemented as a guessing game. The computer generates a random number between 1 and 16,000 and then generates a "guess" at what the number could be. Each guess divides in half the range of potential numbers containing the target value. For example, after guessing 8000 and being told the guess is too low, we know that the mystery number must be between 8001 and 16,000. Thus we have cut the range of numbers in half. It never fails to amaze people how quickly this binary search (called binary because it divides the group by two) works.

Like the Shell sort, the binary search can be applied to other information—numerical and character—in a wide range of data structures. The only requirement is that the structures must be ordered.

The program contains options that allow you to get an automatic demonstration of its operation. The actual code is straightforward and self-documenting.

```
PROGRAM BinarySearchLogic;
    {Change Maximum from 10 to 100, 200, 500, 1000, 5000, 10000
     and 15000 and see how many additional passes it takes as the
     data base gets larger.}

{Suggestion: add the timer program to this one and let it run
 automatically to see just how fast it is on an ORDERED grouping.}

{$I ROUTINE.INC}
VAR
   Minimum, Maximum, UnknownNumber, Turns, Guess, Range :INTEGER;
   Found : Boolean;

PROCEDURE Initialize;
BEGIN
  CLRSCR;
  Found := FALSE;
  Turns := 1;
  Guess := 0;
  Minimum := 0;
  Maximum := 16000; {Why should you avoid integers larger than 16383?}
  UnknownNumber := RANDOM (Maximum);
  WRITELN ('I am thinking of a number between 1 and ',Maximum,'
           Can you guess it?');
END;

PROCEDURE PrintStatus;
BEGIN
  Range := (Maximum - Minimum);
  WRITELN ('You now know that the target must be between ',
           Minimum:5,' and ', Maximum:5, '.');
  WRITELN ('Your next guess will be the midpoint of this
           ',Range:5, ' character range.')
END;

PROCEDURE GetGuess;
BEGIN
{Comment out the next line for an automatic demonstration.}
  WaitForAnyKey;
  Guess := (Minimum + Maximum) DIV 2;  {Determines midpoint of range.}
  WRITELN ('Your guess is ',Guess)
END;

PROCEDURE GetAndEvaluateGuess;
BEGIN
  GetGuess;
  WHILE NOT Found DO
    BEGIN
      IF Guess = UnknownNumber THEN
        BEGIN

          WRITELN ('The unknown number was ',UnknownNumber);
          Found := TRUE
        END;
```

Figure 2.10: The program BINARY.PAS to demonstrate the high-speed binary search of an ordered data structure.

```
      IF Guess < UnknownNumber THEN   {Unknown number is in upper
                                       half of range.}
        BEGIN
          WRITELN ('Too low.');
          Turns := Turns + 1;
          Minimum := Guess;  {New range becomes top half of old range.}
          PrintStatus;
          GetGuess
        END;

          IF Guess > UnknownNumber THEN  {Unknown number is in
                                          lower half of range.}
            BEGIN
              WRITELN ('Too high');
              Turns := Turns + 1;
              Maximum := Guess;     {New range becomes bottom half
                                     of old range.}
              PrintStatus;
              GetGuess
            END;

  END; {While}
END; {GetAndEvaluateGuess}

BEGIN
  Initialize;
  GetAndEvaluateGuess;
  WRITELN ('It took', Turns:3, ' tries to find the number.');
  WRITELN;
END.
```

Figure 2.10: (continued)

3 Simple Games

Introduction

Many programmers find it more fun to write computer games than to play them. This is understandable because, perhaps even more than serious commercial programming applications, game programs seem to invite the widest range of creativity and provide a field for exercising the freest imagination. The opportunity to use sound, graphics, random numbers, and clever screen messages makes writing games a popular programming niche. For many programmers who did their initial game programming with BASIC, however, the speed limitations of the BASIC interpreter limited the range of practical games to fairly simple ones. Particularly in the case of adventure games, the increased time it took to parse a large command repertoire made the most ambitious and thought-provoking games intolerably slow to run.

As it does for so many other applications, Turbo excels for game programming with its lightning-like speed, its support for both string handling and keyboard interaction, and its comprehensive set of graphics and sound options.

The two simple programs presented here attempt only to show some of the facets of game programming in Turbo. Most of the programs in this chapter and the next were adapted from *Apple Pascal Games* by Douglas Hergert and Joseph Kalash (SYBEX, 1981). This is the de facto source book for Pascal games regardless of the dialect. In addition to containing listings for dozens of computer games of all degrees of difficulty, it includes exceptionally lucid explanations of the programming techniques used. Anyone wanting fuller explanations of the techniques used here, as well as other programming ideas, will find *Apple Pascal Games* to be a great resource.

The programs here, however, have been modified to avoid the peculiarities of the Apple dialect and to exploit the capabilities of Turbo. They have also been revised to provide more internal documentation. Even more importantly, they have been modified to exploit many of the techniques and routines covered in the first two chapters of this book.

A Twinkling Screen—TWINKLE.PAS

T*WINKLE.PAS* is shown in Figure 3.1. The program fills the screen, in random order, with asterisks and then removes the asterisks in an equally random order. Obvious variations on this program include adding sound, filling the screen with a variety of different symbols, adding color to only certain symbols, and interleaving painting and removing images to create a truly "twinkling" effect.

The version of the program shown here is relatively simple, yet uses some clever programming techniques with applications outside game programming.

The program first creates an ordered array of every possible character position on the screen. Each screen position is represented by a simple record containing its *x* and *y* coordinates.

Once the ordered array is complete, an elegantly simple routine called *MixUpArrayContents* operates almost like a backwards Shell sort. It proceeds to take each successive array position and swap its contents with the contents of another, randomly chosen, array index.

This routine can be applied to "shuffling" a deck of cards or mixing up a group of questions for a computer quiz.

Once an array that contains every screen position (but in a random sequence) has been created, it is a simple matter to process the array, painting a character at each location. Procedure *Fill* does the painting for us. To "unpaint" the screen the main program calls *Fill* a second time, filling each position with a blank instead of an asterisk.

```
PROGRAM Twinkle;
{This is Doug's best twinkle!!!}
CONST
  ScreenSize    = 1920;   {Maximum number of positions on the screen}
  HorizontalMax = 79;
  VerticalMax   = 23;
TYPE
  Position = RECORD
    HorizontalLoc : 0..HorizontalMax;
    VerticalLoc   : 0..VerticalMax
  END;
  Index = 1..ScreenSize;
VAR
  Screen : ARRAY [Index] OF Position;


PROCEDURE InitializeScreen;
VAR
   ScreenIndex : INTEGER;
   Horizontal : 0..HorizontalMax;
   Vertical : 0..VerticalMax;
BEGIN
  CLRSCR;
  ScreenIndex := 1;
  FOR Horizontal := 0 TO HorizontalMax DO
    FOR Vertical := 0 TO VerticalMax DO
    BEGIN
      Screen [ScreenIndex].HorizontalLoc := Horizontal;
      Screen [ScreenIndex].VerticalLoc := Vertical;
      ScreenIndex := ScreenIndex + 1
    END
END; {InitializeScreen}


PROCEDURE MixUpArrayContents;
  {Swaps the contents of randomly chosen pairs of array cells.}
  {This technique is useful for shuffling cards and
   initializing other random or pseudo-random collections.}
VAR
  I : Index;
  Temp : Position;
  Rnd : Index;
BEGIN
  FOR I := 1 TO ScreenSize DO
  BEGIN
    Rnd := RANDOM (ScreenSize) + 1;
    Temp := Screen [Rnd];
    Screen [Rnd] := Screen [I];
    Screen [I] := Temp;
  END
END;  { MixUpArrayContents }

PROCEDURE Fill (Ch : CHAR);
VAR
  I : Index;
```

Figure 3.1: The program TWINKLE.PAS randomly fills the screen with stars and then removes them.

```
BEGIN
  FOR I := 1 TO ScreenSize DO
  BEGIN
    GOTOXY (Screen[I].HorizontalLoc, Screen[I].VerticalLoc);
    WRITE (Ch);
    DELAY (RANDOM (10));  {Adds a little interest.}
  END
END; {Fill}

BEGIN
  InitializeScreen;
  MixUpArrayContents;
  Fill ('*');
  MixUpArrayContents;
  Fill (' ')
END.
```

Figure 3.1: (continued)

A Dice Game—DICE.PAS

Figure 3.2 contains a program called *DICE.PAS*. This is a version of Chuckaluck, which uses techniques common to all computer dice games and all computer betting games. It also contains an aptly-named procedure, *WindowDressing*, that demonstrates the use of the *TITLE.INC* include file as a painless way to add a professional-looking title screen. The program also makes extensive use of the user-interaction routines (like *WaitForAnyKey* and *YesOrNo*) to streamline interaction with the user. The operation of the game is very simple—a guess is solicited from the player, three random numbers are generated to represent the values of three dice, and the player's winnings or losses are calculated based on the values of the dice.

The game is quite addictive, and the program can be easily modified to play many of the other traditional dice games. It is included here particularly to demonstrate user interaction, an important aspect of which is checking input. Notice how the *GetNumber* routine in the program is used to filter out illegal guesses.

```
PROGRAM ChuckALuck;
{$I Title.inc}
{$I Routine.inc}
CONST
  StartMoney   =  1000;
  MaxDie       =     6;
  MinDie       =     1;
  NumDie       =     3;
  EvenMoney    =     1;
  DoubleMoney  =     2;
  TripleMoney  =     3;
TYPE
  Str80  = STRING[80];
VAR
  Money  : INTEGER;
  Bet    : INTEGER;
  Guess  : MinDie..MaxDie;
  Ch     : CHAR;
  EachDie: 1..NumDie;
  Matched: 0..NumDie;

PROCEDURE GiveInstructions;
BEGIN
  CLRSCR;
  WRITELN;
  WRITELN ('You choose a number between 1 and 6.');
  WRITELN ('I roll three dice.');
  WRITELN;
  WRITELN ('If you match 1, you get even money.');
  WRITELN;
  WRITELN ('If you match 2 dice you get double your bet.');
  WRITELN;
  WRITELN ('If you match all three, you get triple.');
  WRITELN;
  WRITELN ('Of course, if nothing matches, you lose your bet.');
  WRITELN;
  WaitForAnyKey
END;


FUNCTION GetNumber (Question:Str80; Min, Max : INTEGER) : INTEGER;
VAR
  Integ : INTEGER;           { intermediate result }
BEGIN
  WRITE (Question);
  READLN (Integ);
  IF (Integ < Min) OR (Integ > Max) THEN
  BEGIN
    WRITELN ('only numbers between ',Min,' and ',Max,' are allowed.');
    GetNumber := GetNumber (Question,Min,Max)
  END
  ELSE
    GetNumber := Integ
END;  { GetNumber }
```

Figure 3.2: The program DICE.PAS to play Chuckaluck.

```
FUNCTION Rolldie: INTEGER;
VAR
  Dievalue : MinDie..MaxDie;
BEGIN
  DieValue := Mindie + RANDOM (Maxdie);
  WRITE (DieValue:4,'  ');
  RollDie := DieValue
END; { RollDie }

PROCEDURE WindowDressing;
BEGIN
  CLRSCR;
  PrintMessage ('CHUCK',1);
  PrintMessage ('-A-',9);
  PrintMessage ('LUCK',17);
  GOTOXY (22,24);
  WaitForAnyKey;
  CLRSCR;
END;


BEGIN
  WindowDressing;
  Money := StartMoney;
  IF (YesOrNo ('Want instructions? ')) THEN GiveInstructions;
  CLRSCR;
  REPEAT
    WRITELN;
    WRITELN ('You have $',Money);
    Bet := GetNumber ('How large a bet? ',1,Money);
    Guess := GetNumber ('Pick a number ',MinDie,MaxDie);
    Matched := 0;
    WRITELN ('Diel  Die2  Die3');
    FOR EachDie := 1 TO NumDie DO
      IF RollDie =  Guess THEN
        Matched := Matched + 1;
    WRITELN;
    IF Matched = 1 THEN
    BEGIN
      WRITELN ('You won $',Bet * EvenMoney);
      Money := Money + Bet * EvenMoney
    END

    ELSE
    IF Matched = 2 THEN
    BEGIN
      WRITELN ('you won $',Bet * DoubleMoney);
      Money := Money + Bet * DoubleMoney
    END

    ELSE
    IF Matched = 3 THEN
    BEGIN
      WRITELN ('You won $',Bet * TripleMoney);
      Money := Money + Bet * TripleMoney
    END
```

Figure 3.2: (continued)

```
    ELSE
    BEGIN
      WRITELN ('You lost $',Bet);
      Money := Money - Bet
    END;
    IF Money > 0 THEN
    BEGIN
      WRITE ('Care to try your luck again? ');
      READ (KBD, Ch);
     END
   UNTIL (Money <= 0) OR (UPCASE (Ch) <> 'Y');
 WRITELN;
 WRITELN ('You leave with $',Money)
END.
```

Figure 3.2: (continued)

4 Advanced Games

Introduction

This chapter contains the listings for three of the most popular computer games—Hunt the Wumpus, Blackjack, and Life. Again, the skeletons of these game programs came from *Apple Pascal Games*, but they include modules and ideas culled from many other sources, as there are hundreds of variations of these three games. Each has probably been written in just about every programming language—and dialect—that there is.

The programs are presented in ascending order of complexity, from a relatively simple, but still far from trivial, version of Wumpus to one of the nicest implementations of Life that I have ever encountered.

Hunt the Wumpus—WUMPUS.PAS

WUMPUS.PAS, shown in Figure 4.1, is a streamlined version of the game, omitting many of the variations on the underground tunnels that characterize some other versions. It is included here primarily because it shows a simple command interpreter. It also demonstrates the technique of copying only selected routines from *ROUTINE.INC* rather than including the entire file. The program is also a good example of self-documentation.

Wumpus can be considered the prehistoric ancestor of today's text adventure games. In Wumpus a player is offered a limited range of moves (movement or shooting an arrow), and the program determines a limited range of consequences (falling into a pit, killing the Wumpus, moving the player, shooting an arrow that misses the target, or interaction with bats). Once you understand this stripped-down version of Wumpus, it is a simple matter to tackle more ambitious games that offer wider ranges of player options and program reactions.

Again, *Apple Pascal Games* contains a good explanation of the basic operation of all three games in this chapter, although the listings here have been modified to be more self-documenting. The WRITELN statements in procedure *DoInstr* summarize the player's options, and each procedure is preceded by a comment describing its operation.

As in all game programs (and most programs with more serious applications), user interaction is important. Note particularly how the procedures *Command, YesOrNo, DoMove,* and *DoQuit* all allow the user to type in responses in upper- or lowercase and also filter out some forms of erroneous input. Similarly, the routine *DoATurn* uses a CASE statement to choose an option based on a player response. It offers perhaps the simplest example of how well Turbo lends itself to game programming in an almost intuitively understandable manner.

```
PROGRAM Wumpus;
CONST
  MaxRooms          = 20;
  MaxBats           = 2;
  MaxPits           = 2;
  NumberOfArrows    = 7;
  Prompt            = '> ';
  TunnelsPerRoom    = 2;
  MOVE              = 'M';
  Quit              = 'Q';
  Shoot             = 'S';
  Help              = '?';
TYPE
  Room = 1..MaxRooms;
  Rooms = SET OF Room;
  UniversalString = STRING[255];
VAR
  Cave         : ARRAY[Room] OF Rooms;
  Player       : Room;
  Wumpus       : Room;
  ArrowsLeft   : INTEGER;
  Quitting     : BOOLEAN;
  Killed       : BOOLEAN;
  WumpusKilled : BOOLEAN;
  Bats         : Rooms;
  Pits         : Rooms;
  CommandSet   : SET OF CHAR;

PROCEDURE WaitForAnyKey;          {Pauses and waits for any key.}
VAR
  AnyKey : CHAR;
BEGIN
  WRITELN ('To continue, please strike any key.');
  READ (KBD, AnyKey)
END;

FUNCTION YesOrNo (PromptMessage : UniversalString) : BOOLEAN;
VAR
  Response : CHAR;
BEGIN
  WRITE(PromptMessage,' (Y/N) ');
  REPEAT
    READ (KBD, Response);
  UNTIL Response IN ['Y','y','N','n'];
  WRITE (Response);
  YesOrNo := Response IN ['Y','y']
END;

FUNCTION Dup (HowMany : INTEGER; WhatSymbol : CHAR) : UniversalString;
VAR
  Temp : UniversalString;  {Holds pattern as it is created}
  I    : BYTE;             {For Counter}
BEGIN
  Temp := '';
  FOR I := 1 TO HowMany DO
    Temp := Temp + WhatSymbol;
  Dup := Temp
END;
```

Figure 4.1: The program WUMPUS.PAS is a straightforward implementation of the popular computer game.

```
FUNCTION Rand (Low, High : INTEGER) : INTEGER;
BEGIN
   Rand := Low + RANDOM (High-Low+1)
END;


PROCEDURE DoInstr;
BEGIN
  WRITELN;
  WRITELN('Your mission, should you desire to accept it, is to
             hunt for the');
  WRITELN('Wumpus in his cave. To succeed, you must shoot it
             with one of your');
  WRITELN(NumberOfArrows:1,' arrows. If you shoot into a room
             which is not directly connected to');
  WRITELN('yours, the arrow will bounce to one of the rooms that
             does connect.');
  WRITELN('The bats in the cave may pick you up and place you in
             a different');
  WRITELN('room. If you enter a room which has a pit, you will
             fall into it.');
  WRITELN('If the Wumpus finds you or you run out of arrows, you
             lose.');
  WRITELN;
  WRITELN ('To move, shoot, or quit, type M, S, or Q.  ? will get
             you some');
  WRITELN ('help.  Be sure to use capital letters.');
  WRITELN;
  WaitForAnyKey
END;


PROCEDURE AskInstruct;
BEGIN
  CLRSCR;
  IF YesOrNo ('Do you want instructions? ') THEN DoInstr
END;

{This procedure makes a tunnel connection between two rooms.}

PROCEDURE AddTunnel (From, Dest : Room);
BEGIN
   Cave[From] := Cave[From] + [Dest];
   Cave[Dest] := Cave[Dest] + [From]
END;

{The next procedure makes a reasonably random maze. For each
 room, it tries to make 3 new tunnels. If a tunnel already exists
 in that direction, another digging that way is not made.}

PROCEDURE MakeMaze;
VAR
  CurrentRoom, TunnelTo, NewTunnel : Room;
BEGIN
  FOR CurrentRoom := 2 TO MaxRooms DO
    AddTunnel(currentRoom, currentRoom-1);
  FOR CurrentRoom := 3 TO MaxRooms DO
```

Figure 4.1: (continued)

```
     BEGIN
     NewTunnel := Rand(1, CurrentRoom-1);
     IF NOT NewTunnel IN Cave[CurrentRoom] THEN
       AddTunnel(CurrentRoom, NewTunnel)
     END
END; {MakeMaze}

PROCEDURE Describe;
VAR
    i : Room;
BEGIN
  WRITELN('You are in Room ',Player:1);
  WRITE('There are tunnels leading to rooms');
  FOR i := 1 TO MaxRooms DO
      IF i IN Cave[Player] THEN
         WRITE(' ',i:1);
  WRITELN;
   IF (player IN Cave[Wumpus]) OR ((Cave[Player] * Cave[Wumpus])
               <> []) THEN
      WRITELN('I smell a Wumpus.');
   IF Cave[Player] * Bats <> [] THEN
      WRITELN('I hear bats.');
   IF Cave[Player] * Pits <> [] THEN
      WRITELN('I feel a draft.')
END; {Describe}

FUNCTION Command : CHAR;
VAR
  Ch : CHAR;
BEGIN
  Describe;
  REPEAT
    WRITE (Prompt);
    READLN(Ch);
    IF NOT (Ch IN CommandSet) THEN
      BEGIN
      WRITELN(' Type ? for instructions.')
      END;
  UNTIL Ch IN Commandset;
  Command := Ch
END;

{The next procedure moves the Wumpus and sees if it went to the
 same room as the player. If so, he's dead.}

PROCEDURE CheckWump;
VAR
  NewWumpRoom : Room;
BEGIN
  NewWumpRoom := Rand(1, MaxRooms);
  IF (NewWumpRoom IN Cave[Wumpus]) THEN
    Wumpus := NewWumpRoom;
  IF (Wumpus = Player) THEN
    BEGIN
      WRITELN('Look Out!! The Wumpus got you.');
      WRITELN('Better luck next time.');
      Killed := TRUE
    END;
END; {CheckWump}
```

Figure 4.1: (continued)

```
{CheckBats: If the player is in a room with bats, they will pick
 him up and move him to another room (which will not have bats in
 it). }

PROCEDURE CheckBats;
VAR
  FlewTo : Room;
BEGIN
  IF Player IN Bats THEN
    BEGIN
    REPEAT
      FlewTo := Rand(1,MaxRooms)
    UNTIL (NOT (FlewTo IN (Bats + Pits))) AND (FlewTo <> Wumpus);
    WRITELN('A superbat picked you up and carried you off.');
    Player := FlewTo
    END
END;

{ CheckPits determines if the player fell into a pit.}

PROCEDURE CheckPits;
BEGIN
  IF NOT Killed AND (Player IN pits) THEN
    BEGIN
    WRITELN('Don''t do that!! Too late, you fell into a pit.');
    WRITELN('You should be more careful.');
    Killed := TRUE
    END
END; {CheckPits}

{RandRoom returns a random room number in the range limited by
 the set argument.}

FUNCTION RandRoom ( LimitedTo : Rooms) : INTEGER;
VAR
  APossibility : Room;
BEGIN
  REPEAT
    APossibility := Rand(1, MaxRooms);
  UNTIL APossibility IN LimitedTo;
  RandRoom := APossibility;
END;

{DoShoot: The player tries to shoot the Wumpus by listing the rooms
 that he wants to shoot through. If the rooms do not match the list,
 the arrow bounces randomly to a connecting tunnel.}

PROCEDURE DoShoot;
VAR
  NextRoom, LastRoom : Room;
BEGIN
   LastRoom := Player;
   WHILE NOT EOLN DO
     BEGIN
       WRITE('where ');
       READLN(NextRoom);
       IF Wumpus = NextRoom THEN
         WumpusKilled := TRUE
```

Figure 4.1: (continued)

```
        ELSE IF Player = NextRoom THEN
          Killed := TRUE;
        IF NOT (NextRoom IN Cave[LastRoom]) THEN
          NextRoom := RandRoom(Cave[LastRoom]);
       LastRoom := NextRoom
    END; {While}
    ArrowsLeft := ArrowsLeft - 1;
    IF Killed THEN
       WRITELN('You klutz! You just shot yourself.')
    ELSE IF WumpusKilled THEN
       WRITELN('Congratulations! You slew the fearsome Wumpus.')
    ELSE IF ArrowsLeft = 0 THEN
       WRITELN('You ran out of arrows.')
END; {DoShoot}

{ DoMove: Player's move must be to an adjacent room.}

PROCEDURE DoMove;
VAR
  Dest : Room;
BEGIN
  WRITE('To ');
  READLN(Dest);
  IF NOT (Dest IN [1..MaxRooms]) THEN
    WRITELN('There is no Room # ', Dest)
  ELSE IF NOT (Dest IN cave[player]) THEN
    WRITELN('I see no tunnel to room # ',Dest)
  ELSE
    Player := Dest;
    CheckBats;
    CheckWump;
    CheckPits
  END;

  { DoQuit: Asks if the player really wants to quit. }

  PROCEDURE DoQuit;
  VAR
     Answer : CHAR;

  BEGIN
    WRITELN;
    WRITE('Do you really want to quit now? ');
    READLN(Answer);
    Quitting := Answer IN ['y','Y']
  END;

  PROCEDURE DoATurn(Action : CHAR);
  BEGIN
     CASE Action OF
        MOVE   : Domove;
        Shoot : Doshoot;
        Quit  : Doquit;
        Help  : Doinstr;
        END {Case}
  END; {DoATurn}

  { GameOver: Returns TRUE if the game is over.}
```

Figure 4.1: (continued)

```
FUNCTION Gameover : BOOLEAN;
BEGIN
   Gameover := Quitting OR Killed OR WumpusKilled OR (ArrowsLeft = 0)
END;

{Initialize: Generates a random maze and the positions of the player,
 Wumpus, and Bats. Make sure that the player doesn't start
 with the Wumpus.}

 PROCEDURE Initialize;
 VAR
   i : INTEGER;
 BEGIN
   CLRSCR;
   FOR i := 1 TO MaxRooms DO
     Cave[i] := [];
   Bats := [];
   Pits := [];
   MakeMaze;
   Wumpus := Rand(1, MaxRooms);
   FOR i := 1 TO MaxBats DO
     Bats := Bats + [Rand(1, MaxRooms)];
   FOR i := 1 TO Maxpits DO
     Pits := Pits + [Rand(1, MaxRooms)];
   REPEAT
     Player := Rand(1, MaxRooms);
   UNTIL (Player <> Wumpus) AND NOT (Player IN Pits)
   AND NOT (Player IN Bats);
   Quitting := FALSE;
   Killed := FALSE;
   WumpusKilled := FALSE;
   ArrowsLeft := NumberOfArrows;
   CommandSet := [MOVE, Shoot, Quit, Help];
END; {Initialize}

BEGIN
   WRITELN('Welcome to Wumpus!!');
   AskInstruct;
   Initialize;
   REPEAT
      DoATurn (command);
   UNTIL GameOver;
END.
```

Figure 4.1: (continued)

BLACK.PAS

The version of Blackjack shown in Figure 4.2 takes the basic version of Blackjack and, with just a few extra lines of code, dresses up the bare-bones program with graphics and a showy title. *TITLE.INC* again serves as a quick routine for producing titles. The game also uses the technique of randomly swapping the contents of locations within an array, the same concept illustrated in *TWINKLE.PAS.*

One wrinkle in this version of Blackjack is that the routine *Initialize* uses the card suit symbols from the IBM PC's extended character set to show the card suits graphically rather than with words. If your computer does not support these characters, it is a simple matter to substitute letters or words for the graphic symbols (ASCII 3 to 6) used here.

Unlike Wumpus with its simple alternatives, Blackjack offers the programmer the challenge of tracking sequential events. Thus, one must keep track of a diminishing deck; and comparisons and calculations must be repeated with the dealing of each successive card. Again, the modularity of Turbo shines here with the clearly-defined routines *CountCards, DealHands, PlayerTakes, DealerTakes,* and *WhoWon* each helping to break down a fairly complex game into discrete, easy-to-handle operations.

```
PROGRAM BjGame;
{$I TITLE.INC}
CONST
  DeckSize    = 52;
  MaxHandSize = 5;
  MinCards    = 5;
  DealerStays = 17;
  Busted      = 21;
  StartAmount = 100;
  MinBet      = 2;
  MaxBet      = 200;

TYPE
  CardSuit = (Spades, Hearts, Clubs, Diamonds);
  CardValue = (Deuce, Three, Four, Five, Six, Seven, Eight, Nine,
               Ten, Jack, Queen, King, Ace);
  CardState = (Picked, InDeck);
  Card = RECORD
           Suit : CardSuit;
           Value : CardValue;
           State : CardState
         END;
  Hand = ARRAY [1..MaxHandSize] OF Card;

VAR
   Deck         : ARRAY[1..DeckSize] OF Card;
   CardsLeft    : INTEGER;
   SuitName     : ARRAY[CardSuit] OF STRING[8];
   ValueName    : ARRAY[CardValue] OF STRING[5];
   CountValue   : ARRAY[CardValue] OF INTEGER;
   Player       : Hand;
   Dealer       : Hand;
   Money        : INTEGER;
   Bet          : INTEGER;
   CurCard      : INTEGER;
   AnyChar     : Char;
(*
 { Write the suit and value of a card.}

PROCEDURE PrintCard(ACard: Card);
BEGIN
   WRITE('the ',ValueName[ACard.Value]);
   WRITELN(' of ',SuitName[ACard.Suit])
END;
*)


PROCEDURE PrintCard(ACard: Card);
BEGIN
  WRITE(' ',ValueName[ACard.Value]);
  WRITELN(' ',SuitName[ACard.Suit])
END;


 { Asks for instructions.}
```

Figure 4.2: The program BLACK.PAS to play the ever-popular game of Blackjack.

```
PROCEDURE Instructions;

VAR
  Response : CHAR;

BEGIN
  WRITELN(' ':15,'Blackjack for one');
  WRITELN('Do you want instructions?  [Y/N] ');
  READ (KBD, Response);
  IF (Response = 'y') OR (Response = 'Y') THEN
      BEGIN
      WRITELN('This program plays a simple version of Blackjack.
Neither');
      WRITELN('splitting, nor modification of the bet after the
hand has');
      WRITELN('been dealt is allowed.');
      END;
   WRITELN
END; {Instructions}


 { Returns true if the card c is in the hand.}


FUNCTION InHand(c: Card; Whose: Hand): BOOLEAN;

VAR
   HandIndex : INTEGER;

BEGIN
  InHand := FALSE;
  FOR HandIndex := 1 TO MaxHandSize DO
    IF ((c.Suit = Whose[HandIndex].Suit) AND
      (c.Value = Whose[HandIndex].Value)) THEN
      BEGIN
        InHand := TRUE;
        END
END; {InHand}

{ Returns a random index into the deck.}

FUNCTION RandCard(l: INTEGER) : INTEGER;
BEGIN
  RandCard := 1 + RANDOM(l);
END;

{ Removes all cards from the argument hand.}

PROCEDURE ClearHand(VAR AHand: Hand);
VAR
  HandIndex : INTEGER;


BEGIN
  FOR HandIndex := 1 TO MaxHandSize DO
  AHand[HandIndex].State := InDeck;
END;
```

Figure 4.2: (continued)

```
{ Initialize the names of the suits and values.}

PROCEDURE Initialize;
VAR
  i       : INTEGER;
  CardVal : CardValue;

BEGIN
  Instructions;
  ClearHand(Player);
  ClearHand(Dealer);
  Money := StartAmount;
  CardsLeft := 0;
  i := 2;
  FOR CardVal := Deuce TO Ten DO

    BEGIN
      CountValue[CardVal] := i;
      i := i + 1
        END;
  FOR CardVal := Jack TO King DO
    CountValue[CardVal] := 10;
  CountValue[Ace] := 11;

  ValueName[Deuce]  := ' 2';
  ValueName[Three]  := ' 3';
  ValueName[Four]   := ' 4';
  ValueName[Five]   := ' 5';
  ValueName[Six]    := ' 6';
  ValueName[Seven]  := ' 7';
  ValueName[Eight]  := ' 8';
  ValueName[Nine]   := ' 9';
  ValueName[Ten]    := '10';
  ValueName[Jack]   := ' J';
  ValueName[Queen]  := ' Q';
  ValueName[King]   := ' K';
  ValueName[Ace]    := ' A';
  SuitName[Diamonds] := #4;
  SuitName[Spades]   := #6;  {PC graphic}
  SuitName[Hearts]   := #3;
  SuitName[Clubs]    := #5
END; {Initialize}

{ The next procedure shuffles the cards that are not in either
  player's hand. The initial shuffle does all the cards because
  both hands start empty.}

PROCEDURE Shuffle;
VAR
  ASuit  : CardSuit;
  AValue : CardValue;
  i      : INTEGER;

 { The next procedure exchanges the cards at the two positions
   in the deck.}
```

Figure 4.2: (continued)

```
PROCEDURE SwapCard(First, Second : Integer);
VAR
  TempCard : Card;
BEGIN
  TempCard := Deck[First];
  Deck[First] := Deck[Second];
  Deck[Second] := TempCard
END;

BEGIN
  i := 1;
  FOR ASuit := Spades To Diamonds DO
    FOR AValue := Deuce TO Ace DO
      WITH Deck[i] DO
      BEGIN
      Suit := ASuit;
      Value := AValue;
      IF NOT (InHand(Deck[i], Player) OR InHand(Deck[i], Dealer)) THEN
            BEGIN
              State := InDeck;
              i := i + 1;
            END
       END; {With}
  CurCard := 0;
  CardsLeft := i - 1;
  WRITELN('*** ',CardsLeft:1,' cards left.');
  FOR i := 1 TO CardsLeft DO
    SwapCard(i, RandCard(CardsLeft))
END; {SwapCard}

 { PickCard: Returns the index into the deck of the next card.
 Calls shuffle if deck is nearly finished.


FUNCTION PickCard : INTEGER;

BEGIN
  IF CardsLeft < MinCards THEN
    BEGIN
      WRITELN('Reshuffling ...');
      Shuffle
    END;
  CurCard := CurCard + 1;
  Deck[CurCard].State := Picked;
  CardsLeft := CardsLeft - 1;
  PickCard := CurCard
END; {PickCard}

 {CountCards: Determines the sum of the values in a hand. A
  card's state must be 'picked' for it to be included. Aces are
  assumed to be 11. If the count is over 21 and there are aces in
  it, as many as are needed will be devalued to 1.}


FUNCTION CountCards(Someone: Hand): INTEGER;
VAR
  HandIndex, Sum, NumAces : INTEGER;
```

Figure 4.2: (continued)

```
BEGIN
  Sum := 0;
  NumAces := 0;
  FOR HandIndex := 1 TO MaxHandSize DO
    IF Someone[HandIndex].State = Picked THEN
      WITH Someone[HandIndex] DO
      BEGIN
      IF Value = Ace THEN
        NumAces := NumAces +1;
      Sum := Sum + CountValue[Value]
      END;
  WHILE (NumAces > 0) AND (Sum > Busted) DO
    BEGIN
      NumAces := NumAces - 1;
      Sum := Sum - 10
      END;
  CountCards := Sum
END;

{ The next function returns TRUE if the argument Hand is a
  blackjack. }

FUNCTION BlackJack(Someone: Hand): BOOLEAN;
BEGIN
  BlackJack := ((CountValue[Someone[1].Value] = 10) AND
                (CountValue[Someone[2].Value] = 11)) OR
               ((CountValue[Someone[1].Value] = 11) AND
                (CountValue[Someone[2].Value] = 10))
END;


PROCEDURE GetBet;
CONST
  BetPrompt = 'Size of bet (0 to end)? ';
BEGIN
  WRITE (BetPrompt);
  READLN (Bet);
  WHILE NOT (Bet IN [0,MinBet..MaxBet]) OR (Bet > Money) DO
    BEGIN
      WRITE ('A bet must be between ');
      WRITELN (MinBet:1,' and ',MaxBet:1);
      WRITELN ('and must be no larger than the amount of money');
      WRITELN ('you have. Enter 0 to leave.');
      WRITE (BetPrompt)
      READLN(Bet);
    END;
   IF Bet = 0 THEN
     BEGIN
       WRITELN('You have quit with $',Money:1,'.');
       HALT;
   END
END; {GetBet}

{ DealHands: Deals the cards to both participants for this hand. }

PROCEDURE DealHands;
BEGIN
  Player[1] := Deck[PickCard];
```

Figure 4.2: (continued)

```
  Dealer[1] := Deck[PickCard];
  Player[2] := Deck[PickCard];
  Dealer[2] := Deck[PickCard];
  WRITE('                You drew:');
  PrintCard(Player[1]);
  WRITE('                          ');
  PrintCard(Player[2]);
  WRITELN;
  WRITELN('         Your count is ',CountCards(Player));
  WRITELN;
  WRITELN;
  WRITE('The dealer''s up card is:');
  PrintCard(Dealer[2])
END;

{ PlayerTakes: Asks the player if more cards are wanted. }

PROCEDURE PlayerTakes;
VAR
  AtCard : INTEGER;
  Answer : CHAR;
BEGIN
  AtCard := 3;
  Answer := 'h';
  WHILE (AtCard <= MaxHandSize) AND (CountCards(Player) < Busted)
  AND ((Answer = 'h') OR (Answer = 'H')) DO
     BEGIN
       WRITELN;
       WRITE('Hit or stay? ');
       WRITELN;
       READ (KBD, Answer);
       IF (Answer = 'h') OR (Answer = 'H') THEN
         BEGIN
           Player[AtCard] := Deck[PickCard];
           WRITELN;
           WRITE ('                You drew:');
           PrintCard(Player[AtCard]);
           WRITELN;
           AtCard := AtCard + 1;
           WRITELN('         Your count is ',countcards(player));
         WRITELN
         END {IF}
      END; {WHILE}
   IF (CountCards(Player) < Busted) AND (AtCard > MaxHandSize)
   THEN WRITELN('You can take only ',MaxHandSize:1,' cards.');
END;

PROCEDURE DealerTakes;

VAR
  AtCard : INTEGER;

BEGIN
  WRITE('  Dealer''s hole card is:');
  PrintCard(Dealer[1]);
  AtCard := 3;
  WHILE (AtCard <= MaxHandSize) AND (CountCards(Dealer) < DealerStays) DO
```

Figure 4.2: (continued)

```
    BEGIN
      Dealer[AtCard] := Deck[PickCard];
      WRITE ('           Dealer drew:');
      PrintCard (Dealer[AtCard]);
      AtCard := AtCard + 1;
    END;
END; {DealerTakes}

PROCEDURE WhoWon;

BEGIN
  WRITELN('                    Dealer has ',CountCards(Dealer):1);
  WRITELN;
  IF BlackJack (Dealer) THEN
    BEGIN
      WRITE ('Dealer got a blackjack.');
      Money := Money - Bet;
    END
  ELSE IF BlackJack(Player) THEN
      BEGIN
        WRITE ('Your blackjack wins!');
        Money := Money + Bet;
      END
   ELSE IF CountCards(Player) > Busted THEN
      BEGIN
        WRITE('You busted.');
        IF CountCards(Dealer) > Busted THEN
          WRITE(' So did the dealer. No payout.')
        ELSE
          Money := Money - Bet;
      END
   ELSE IF CountCards(Dealer) > Busted THEN
      BEGIN
        WRITE('Dealer busts.');
        Money := Money + Bet;
      END
  ELSE IF CountCards(Dealer) = CountCards(Player) THEN
    WRITE('Push.')
  ELSE IF CountCards(Dealer) > CountCards(Player) THEN
    Money := Money - Bet
  ELSE
    Money := Money + Bet;
  WRITELN(' You now have $',money:1)
END; {WhoWon}

BEGIN
  CLRSCR;
  PrintMessage ('BLACKJACK',8);
  GOTOXY (22,24);
  WRITELN ('Press any key to continue');
  READ (KBD, AnyChar);
  CLRSCR;
  Initialize;
  Shuffle;
  REPEAT
    GetBet;
```

Figure 4.2: (continued)

```
    CLRSCR;
    DealHands;
    IF NOT BlackJack(Player) THEN
      PlayerTakes;
    DealerTakes;
    WhoWon;
    ClearHand(Player);
    ClearHand(Dealer);
  UNTIL Money <= 0;
  WRITELN('You have run out of money.')
END.
```

Figure 4.2: (continued)

The Game of Life—BESTLIFE.PAS

The program called *BESTLIFE.PAS*, shown in Figure 4.3, is an implementation of Life—surely one of the most popular and intriguing of all computer games. A particularly nice feature of this implementation is that it is very fast. In fact, it is one of the fastest versions available on a personal computer. Thus, it is inherently more entertaining than slower versions. Not only is the program fast, but in the main loop of the program there is a provision for the player to slow down or speed up the program operation. The program also uses color, has a flashy title screen, contains a brief but informative instruction screen, and even provides for a sample game for new users who are not sure about entering a series of cell coordinates.

The basic operation of the game is conceptually simple (read the instructions in the listing for an explanation of the premise of the game), but the programming is not immediately obvious. Unlike any of the previous games except *TWINKLE, BESTLIFE* is very much concerned with screen "real estate" and must always be aware of the screen edges as limits on the growth and movement of colonies. As each generation is spawned, the program must first check to keep the colony within bounds. After that, it is a process of examining a cell. Based on the pattern of its current neighbors, the program must decide whether to paint the cell in the next generation as a live character (the listing uses ASCII #4, which is a diamond on the IBM PC) or as a dead cell, with a space. Incidentally, it is surprising how different the game looks when you substitute a different graphic symbol for the live character.

The logic of the game has been written up in many sources, and *Apple Pascal Games* has a good explanation of the decision process.

Even without getting bogged down in the intricacies of this program, you can have a great deal of fun just playing with it. And all true Life fans keep a journal of their best sets of starting coordinates.

```
PROGRAM LIFE;
{$I Routine.inc}
{$I Title.inc}
{$I+}
CONST Height = 24;
      Width  = 80;
      MinBound = -1;
      Lively = #4;    {Try other characters for different effects.}
      Deadly = ' ';

TYPE  State = (Alive, Dead);
      Cell = RECORD
               LooksLikeItIs: State;
               Nearby: INTEGER
             END;
      Edges = RECORD Left, Right, Top, Bottom: INTEGER END;
      ScreenLine = STRING[80];

VAR   Board: ARRAY[MinBound..Height] OF ARRAY[MinBound..Width] OF Cell;
      Population, Births, Deaths: INTEGER;
      Ch: CHAR;
      Quit: BOOLEAN;
      Pause: INTEGER;
      Edge: Edges;


FUNCTION Min(a,b: INTEGER):INTEGER;
BEGIN
  IF a<=b THEN Min:=a ELSE Min:=b
END;  {Min}

FUNCTION Max(a,b: INTEGER):INTEGER;
BEGIN
  IF a>=b THEN Max:=a ELSE Max:=b
END;  {Max}

PROCEDURE ResetEdges;
BEGIN
  Edge.Top:=Height-1;
  Edge.Right:=MinBound+1;
  Edge.Left:=Width-1;
  Edge.Bottom:=MinBound+1
END;  {ResetEdges}

PROCEDURE Instructions;
VAR Ch: CHAR;

  PROCEDURE LifeStory;
  BEGIN
    CLRSCR;
    WRITE('Life simulates the growth of a colony of animalcules in a "');
    WRITELN(Width-1:1,' by ',Height-1:1,' World".');
    WRITELN;
    WRITELN('Whether a cell is born, lives or dies depends on the number
 of living');
    WRITELN('animalcules near by.  If a cell is empty and has exactly 3
 neighbors, it');
```

Figure 4.3: The program BESTLIFE.PAS, which is a fast Turbo implementation of LIFE.

```
    WRITELN('will be born in the next generation.  If it is alive and
has 2 or 3');
    WRITELN('neighbors, it will stay alive.  Otherwise, it either
dies of loneliness');
    WRITELN('or suffocates from overcrowding.');
    WRITELN;
    WRITELN('You type in the starting pattern, giving the XY location
of each cell.');
    WRITELN('When you enter X Y be sure to leave a space between the
numbers.  When');
    WRITELN('you are through seeding a colony, enter a -1 to begin the
generations.');
    WRITELN('The < key speeds things up a bit, the > key slows things
down.  In the');
    WRITELN('good old days at M.I.T., this game was played with pencil
& graph paper.');
    WRITELN;
    WRITELN ('For a demo game, type a -2 as the first number');

    GOTOXY(1,22);
    WaitForAnyKey;
  END;  {LifeStory}

BEGIN
  WRITELN;
  IF YesOrNo ('Would you like instructions for Life?') THEN
    LifeStory;
  CLRSCR
END;  {Instructions}

PROCEDURE Initialize;
VAR Down, Across: INTEGER;
BEGIN
  FOR Down:=MinBound TO Height DO
    FOR Across:=MinBound TO Width DO
      BEGIN
        Board[Down,Across].LooksLikeItIs := Dead;
        Board[Down,Across].Nearby := 0
      END;
  ResetEdges
END;  {Initialize}

PROCEDURE Limits(x,y: INTEGER);
BEGIN
  WITH Edge DO
    BEGIN
      Left:=Min(Left,x);
      Right:=Max(Right,x);
      Top:=Min(Top,y);
      Bottom:=Max(Bottom,y)
    END
END; {Limits}

PROCEDURE ClearNearby;
VAR Down, Across: INTEGER;
BEGIN
  FOR Down:=Edge.Top-1 TO Edge.Bottom+1 DO
```

Figure 4.3: (continued)

```
  PROCEDURE ReprintTopLine;
  VAR Across:INTEGER;
  BEGIN
    GOTOXY(1,1);
    FOR Across:=MinBound+1 TO Width-1 DO
      IF Board[MinBound+1][Across].LooksLikeItIs = Dead
        THEN WRITE(Deadly)
        ELSE WRITE(Lively)
  END;  {ReprintTopLine}

BEGIN
  Finished:=FALSE;
  Population:=0;
  GOTOXY(1,1);
  WRITE('Position of Cell #',Population+1:1,' is: ');
  WHILE NOT Finished DO
    BEGIN
      READLN (Across, Down);
               {Works if you leave a space between x and y.}
      IF (Across = -2) THEN
        BEGIN
          CLRSCR;
          WRITELN('*** INPUT ERROR ***');
          WRITE('A Demonstration of LIFE with 9 cells from
32 11 to 41 11:');
          DELAY (1500);
          CLRSCR;
          FOR Across:=31 TO 31+9 DO
            BEGIN
            Limits(Across,10);
            Board[10][Across].LooksLikeItIs:=Alive;
            GOTOXY(Across+1,11);
            WRITE(Lively)
            END;
          FOR Across:=1 TO 128 DO DELAY(5);
          Finished:=TRUE;
          Population:=9
        END {If Across = -2}
      ELSE
        BEGIN
          IF(Down<=MinBound) OR
            (Down>=Height) OR
            (Across<=MinBound) OR
            (Across>=Width) THEN
              Finished:=TRUE
      ELSE WITH Board[Down][Across] DO
        BEGIN
          Limits(Across,Down);
          GOTOXY(Across+1,Down+1);
    FOR Across:=Edge.Left-1 TO Edge.Right+1 DO
      Board[Down,Across].Nearby := 0
END;  {ClearNearby}

PROCEDURE CountNeighbors;
VAR Down, Across, DeltaDown, DeltaCross: INTEGER;
BEGIN
  ClearNearby;
  FOR Down:=Edge.Top-1 TO Edge.Bottom+1 DO
```

Figure 4.3: (continued)

```
    FOR Across:=Edge.Left-1 TO Edge.Right+1 DO
      IF Board[Down][Across].LooksLikeItIs = Alive THEN
        FOR DeltaDown:=-1 TO 1 DO
          FOR DeltaCross:=-1 TO 1 DO

           Board[Down+DeltaDown][Across+DeltaCross].Nearby :=
           Board[Down+DeltaDown][Across+DeltaCross].Nearby + 1
END;  {CountNeighbors}

PROCEDURE UpDate;
VAR Down, Across: INTEGER;
    LocalEdge: Edges;
BEGIN
  Births:=0;
  Deaths:=0;
  LocalEdge:=Edge;
  ResetEdges;
  FOR Down:=Max(MinBound+1,LocalEdge.Top-1) TO
            Min(Height-1,LocalEdge.Bottom+1) DO
  FOR Across:=Max(MinBound+1,LocalEdge.Left-1) TO
              Min(Width-1,LocalEdge.Right+1) DO
     WITH Board[Down][Across] DO
     CASE LooksLikeItIs OF
     Dead:
     IF Nearby=3 THEN
        BEGIN
          LooksLikeItIs:=Alive;
          GOTOXY(Across+1,Down+1);
          WRITE(Lively);
          Limits(Across,Down);
          Births:=Births+1
        END;
     Alive:
     IF (Nearby=3) OR (Nearby=4) THEN Limits(Across,Down)
            ELSE
              BEGIN
                LooksLikeItIs:=Dead;
                GOTOXY(Across+1,Down+1);
                WRITE(Deadly);
                Deaths:=Deaths+1
              END
     END; {case}
  Population:=Population+Births-Deaths;
  GOTOXY(1,1)
END;  {UpDate}

PROCEDURE GetPositions;
VAR Down,Across: INTEGER;
    Finished: BOOLEAN;
          IF LooksLikeItIs = Alive THEN
            BEGIN
              WRITE(Deadly);
              LooksLikeItIs:=Dead;
              Population:=Population-1
            END
          ELSE
            BEGIN
              WRITE(Lively);
```

Figure 4.3: (continued)

```
                LooksLikeItIs:=Alive;
                Population:=Population+1
              END;
            GOTOXY(1,1);
            WRITE('Position of Cell #',Population+1:1,' is: ');
          END {Else with}
        END {Else}
      END; {While}
    ReprintTopLine
  END; {GetPositions}


PROCEDURE WindowDressing;
BEGIN
  TEXTBACKGROUND (4);
  TEXTCOLOR (14);
  CLRSCR;
  PrintMessage ('LIFE',9);
  GOTOXY (22,24);
  WaitForAnyKey;
  CLRSCR;
END;

BEGIN
  WindowDressing;
  REPEAT
    Initialize;
    Instructions;
    GetPositions;
    Pause:=32;
    Quit:=FALSE;
    WHILE NOT Quit DO
      BEGIN
        CountNeighbors;
        UpDate;
        FOR Ch:='A' TO 'Z' DO DELAY(Pause);
        Quit := (Population=0) OR ((Births=0) AND (Deaths=0));
        IF KEYPRESSED THEN
          BEGIN
            READ(KBD,Ch);
            IF Ch IN ['>','.'] THEN Pause:=Min(Pause+16,255)
            ELSE IF Ch IN ['<',','] THEN Pause:=Max(Pause-16,0)
            ELSE Quit:=TRUE
          END
      END; {While}

    GOTOXY(1,22);
    IF Population=0 THEN
    BEGIN
      Beep;
      WRITELN ('This colony has died out.');
    END
      ELSE WRITELN
  UNTIL NOT YesOrNo('Would you like to run LIFE again?')
END.
```

Figure 4.3: (continued)

5 General-Purpose Utility Routines

Introduction

The two programs presented in this chapter show many techniques that can be useful in almost any type of program. The first program provides number conversion between various bases (hexadecimal, decimal, and so on). The second program calculates and plots a three-function biorhythm graph on either the screen or the printer.

Number-Base Conversion— ROUTINE2.INC and NUMCNVRT.PAS

The first group of routines is used to build a number base conversion program that is a handy tool for programmers. This program will convert a wide range of cardinal numbers from one number base to another. For example, it will convert binary to decimal, hexadecimal to octal, decimal to hexadecimal, and so on.

Four routines are combined in the module *ROUTINE2.INC*, listed in Figure 5.1. They are called *TypeBase*, *GetWord*, *ConvertNumberBase*, and *WriteNum*.

The *TypeBase* function returns a string corresponding to the base number specified by the user (that is, base 2 = 'Binary' and base 10 = 'Decimal'). If there is no common name for the base, the string 'Base XX' is returned.

The *GetWord* routine inputs a "word" from the keyboard, which must contain only characters in the specified character set and must be terminated by a carriage return (ASCII 13). Characters not in *Okset* are ignored and are not echoed to the screen. The word is returned in the variable parameter string to the calling statement.

The *ConvertNumberBase* routine converts a string representation of a number in a given base to a decimal real number. An error is returned if an input character is not in the character set for the base specified or if an invalid base is specified. The routine as written will convert numbers in any base from 2 to 16 (binary to hexadecimal).

This conversion routine uses a Turbo Pascal typed constant string named HEXNUM, containing all the characters used in bases 2 through 16, to convert the input value. Each character in the input string is tested for its position in the HEXNUM string, and the position value found is used in the conversion to decimal. For each digit in the input number, the cumulative total of the number is multiplied by the base, and the position value of the current digit is added to the total.

The *WriteNum* procedure is a universal output routine that will write a cardinal (positive whole) number in any specified base. If the base is 2, 8, 10, or 16, the number is formatted according to standard conventions using commas or spaces as appropriate. This procedure includes the *PutNum* and *Format* procedures.

The *PutNum* procedure uses "recursive descent" to convert the real N to a string representing the value of N in the specified base. The conversion is performed from left to right recursively. If this routine is used with the CP/M version of Turbo Pascal, compiler directive {$A-} is required. The routine is accurate at least to 8 hexadecimal digits because of the high accuracy of Turbo Pascal's REAL type. The *Format* procedure formats a string by inserting a formatting character at specified intervals from right to left.

The four routines in *ROUTINE2.INC* are combined to create a programmer's number base conversion program—*NUMCNVRT.PAS*, listed in Figure 5.2. Routines from *ROUTINE.INC* are also used.

```
CONST
  Hexnum: STRING [16] = '0123456789ABCDEF';
TYPE
  CharSet = SET OF CHAR;

FUNCTION TypeBase(Base: INTEGER): UniversalString;
{Returns a string corresponding to the base.}

  VAR
    BaseValue: STRING [2];

  BEGIN
    CASE Base OF
      2:  TypeBase := 'Binary';
      8:  TypeBase := 'Octal';
      10: TypeBase := 'Decimal';
      16: TypeBase := 'Hexadecimal';
      ELSE
        STR(Base, BaseValue);
        TypeBase := 'Base ' + BaseValue;
      END;  {CASE}
  END;   {TypeBase}


PROCEDURE GetWord(VAR InStr: UniversalString; OkSet : CharSet);

{ Input a string containing only OkSet chars; echo good ones.}

  CONST
    CR = #13;
  VAR
    Ch: CHAR;

  BEGIN
    InStr := '';
    REPEAT
      READ(KBD, Ch);
      IF Ch IN OkSet THEN
        BEGIN
        WRITE(UPCASE(Ch));
        InStr := InStr + UPCASE(Ch);
        END;  {IF}
    UNTIL Ch = CR;
    WRITELN;
  END;   {GetWord}


PROCEDURE ConvertNumberBase(InStr: UniversalString;
                            Base: INTEGER;
                            VAR Err: INTEGER;
                            VAR N: REAL);

{Convert a string representing a number in Base to decimal real N.}
{Return ERR = 0 if OK, ERR = 1 if bad char in input, ERR = 2 if }
{Base out of conversion range. }

  VAR
    I: INTEGER;
```

Figure 5.1: The routines in the include file ROUTINE2.INC.

```
  BEGIN
    N := 0.0;
    Err := 0;
    IF (Base <= 16) AND (Base >= 2) THEN
      BEGIN
      FOR I := 1 TO LENGTH(InStr) DO
        IF (InStr[I] IN ['0'..'9', 'A'..'F']) AND
           (POS(InStr[I],Hexnum) - 1 < Base) THEN
          N := N * Base + POS(INSTR[I], Hexnum) - 1
        ELSE
          Err := 1;
      END  {IF Base}
    ELSE
      Err := 2;
  END;   {ConvertNumberBase}


PROCEDURE WriteNum(N: REAL; Base: INTEGER);

{ Write a cardinal number in specified number base and format.}

  CONST
    Space = ' ';
    Comma = ',';

  VAR
    OutString: UniversalString;


  PROCEDURE PutNum(N: REAL; Base: INTEGER; VAR OutStr: UniversalString);
   { Recursive procedure converts N to string representation of number }
   { in Base. }

    BEGIN
      IF N >= 1 THEN
        BEGIN
        PutNum(INT(N / Base), Base, OutStr);
        OutStr := OutStr + (Hexnum[ROUND((N / Base - INT(N / Base)) *
                                                   Base) + 1])
        END;  {IF}
    END;  {PutNum}


PROCEDURE Format(SpaceFormat: INTEGER;
                 FormatChar: CHAR;
                 VAR NumString: UniversalString);
{ Format a string using SpaceFormat spacing and FormatChar delimiter.}

  VAR
    I: INTEGER;

  BEGIN
    I := SpaceFormat;
    WHILE I < LENGTH(NumString) DO
      BEGIN
      INSERT(FormatChar, NumString, LENGTH(NumString) - I + 1);
      I := I + SpaceFormat + 1;
      END;   {WHILE}
  END;  {Format}
```

Figure 5.1: (continued)

```
BEGIN   {WriteNum}
  OutString := '';
  IF N < 1 THEN
    WRITE('0')
  ELSE
    BEGIN
    PutNum(N, Base, OutString);
    CASE Base OF
      2:  Format(4, Space, OutString);
      8:  Format(3, Space, OutString);
      10: Format(3, Comma, OutString);
      16: Format(4, Space, OutString);
      END;   {CASE}
    WRITE(OutString);
    WRITE(' ', TypeBase(Base));
    END;  {ELSE}
END;     {WriteNum}
```

Figure 5.1: (continued)

```
PROGRAM Numcnvrt;

  CONST
    MaxBase = 16;

  VAR
    Base1, Base2: 1..MaxBase;
    Error: INTEGER;
    Num: REAL;
    Done: BOOLEAN;

    {$I ROUTINE.INC }

  VAR
    InString: UniversalString;

    {$I ROUTINE2.INC }

  FUNCTION GetBase(Mess: UniversalString): INTEGER;

    VAR
      Ch: CHAR;
      Base: INTEGER;

    BEGIN
      Write(Mess, ' (B,O,D,H) ');
      REPEAT
        Read(KBD, Ch);
        Ch := UPCASE(Ch);
      UNTIL Ch IN ['B', 'O', 'D', 'H'];
      CASE Ch OF
        'B': Base := 2;
        'O': Base := 8;
        'D': Base := 10;
        'H': Base := 16;
        END;
      WRITELN(TypeBase(Base));
      GetBase := Base;
    END;

  BEGIN
    REPEAT
      CLRSCR;
      WRITELN('Number base conversion program');
      WRITELN;
      WRITELN('Translates numbers from/to:  Binary      (base 2)');
      WRITELN('                             Octal       (base 8)');
      WRITELN('                             Decimal     (base 10)');
      WRITELN('                             Hexadecimal (base 16)');
      WRITELN;
      WRITELN;

   Base1 := GetBase('Enter base for input value:  ');
   Base2 := GetBase('Enter base for output value: ');
   WRITELN;
   WRITE('Enter ', TypeBase(Base1), ' value to convert: ');
   GetWord(InString,['0'..'9','A'..'F','a'..'f']);
```

Figure 5.2: The number-base conversion program NUMCNVRT.PAS.

```
    WRITELN;
    ConvertNumberBase(InString, Basel, Error, Num);
    CASE Error OF
      0: WriteNum(Num, Base2);
      1: WRITELN('Entry error - not a valid ', TypeBase(Basel),
                 ' number.');
      2: WRITELN('Error - not a valid base.');
    END;
    WRITELN;
    WRITELN;
    Done := NOT YesOrNo('More?');
  UNTIL Done;
END.
```

Figure 5.2: (continued)

Plotting Your Biorhythms—BIORYTHM.PAS

Beginning around the turn of the century, several scientists began investigating the possibility that people were subject to one or more natural cycles. After statistical analysis of volumes of empirical data, it was reported that we are all subject (to a greater or lesser extent) to three "universal" cycles or biological rhythms, which affect our daily lives.

These biorhythms are "physical," "emotional," and "intellectual." All three cycles begin when we are born, and continue throughout our lives. The physical cycle has a 23-day period, the emotional cycle a 28-day period, and the intellectual cycle a 33-day period.

The values of each cycle range from positive to crossover or zero to negative to crossover again and back to positive during each period. The graph of this cycle is a sine function. As each cycle has a different period, the relationship between the three cycles is always changing.

When the cycles are positive, you can expect to be "good" in those areas and capable of putting a lot of energy into activities. Negative values indicate a time of regeneration or rebuilding your reserves. Crossovers are a time of possible confusion or error.

Many organizations, including a large Japanese taxi company and some U.S. manufacturing companies, use biorhythms to help schedule personnel for critical tasks by avoiding possible "problem" days indicated by the biorhythm chart. The taxi company, for example, experienced a significant decrease in the number of traffic accidents after drivers were assigned to shop or desk jobs during crossover days.

The *BIORYTHM.PAS* program, listed in Figure 5.3, provides an interesting example of a program which graphs three overlayed curves on either the screen or a printer.

The program is fairly self-explanatory. Procedure *Init* initializes all variables entered by the user. Procedure *PrintHead* displays a description of the program on the screen.

Procedure *PrintBior* calculates the point locations for a single day's graph and displays them on the selected output device. When two or more symbols occupy the same point on the graph, an X is displayed. Otherwise, the symbols for the three cycles (P, I, or E) are displayed, positioned according to their current values. The built-in Turbo procedure INSERT is used to build an output string for later display.

The *Display* procedure is the main program loop, which calculates the biorhythm values for each day up to *LengthOfReport* days and then calls the *PrintBior* routine to display the day's values. Local procedure *CalcBior* calculates the values for a given number of days from birth and *NextDay* calculates the next date for the loop.

The *Start* procedure accepts user entries for name, birth date, chart starting date, and the number of days to display on the chart. Local function *NumDays* determines the number of days from the birth date to the chart starting date. A text-file variable is used to determine whether the output goes to the screen or printer by assigning it to either the CON: or LST: logical device. Finally, the *Display* procedure is called to print the chart.

The main code block simply loops through *Init*, *PrintHead*, and *Start* until no more charts are desired.

```
PROGRAM Biorhythm;

  TYPE
    MonthArray = ARRAY [1..12] OF INTEGER;

  CONST
    Space = ' ';
    Days1: MonthArray = (31, 28, 31, 30, 31, 30, 31, 31, 30, 31, 30, 31);
    Months: ARRAY [1..12] OF STRING [10] =
    ('January', 'February', 'March', 'April', 'May', 'June', 'July',
     'August', 'September', 'October', 'November', 'December');

  VAR
    LengthOfReport, Month1, Month2, Day1, Day2, Year1, Year2,
    TotalDays: INTEGER;
    Physical, Intellectual, Emotional: REAL;
    Name: STRING [30];
    Days: MonthArray;
    Out: TEXT;
    Printout, Done: BOOLEAN;

    {$I ROUTINE.INC }


  PROCEDURE Init;
    BEGIN
      Days := Days1;
      LengthOfReport := 0;
      Month1 := 0;
      Month2 := 0;
      Day1 := 0;
      Day2 := 0;
      Year1 := 0;
      Year2 := 0;
    END;


  PROCEDURE PrintHead;
    BEGIN
      CLRSCR;
      WRITE(Space: 20);
      WRITELN('BIORHYTHM CHART');
      WRITELN;
      WRITELN('Biorhythms are based on the theory that we are
              controlled');
      WRITELN('in part by biological rhythms that begin at our birth.');
      WRITELN;
      WRITELN('These rhythms are PHYSICAL (23-day cycle), ',
              'EMOTIONAL (28-day cycle),');
      WRITELN('and INTELLECTUAL (33-day cycle).  ',
              'The first half of each cycle');
      WRITELN('is considered to be up or high energy period.  ',
              'The last half of');
      WRITELN('each cycle is considered to be down ',
              'or a period of regeneration.');
      WRITELN('The first, last, and middle day of each cycle are ',
              'considered to');
      WRITELN('be critical days - those days in which the biorhythms ',
              'have the');
```

Figure 5.3: The biorhythm program BIORYTHM.PAS.

```
    WRITELN('lowest influence.');
    WRITELN;
    WRITELN('The computer will take your birthdate, ',
            'calculate the number of days');
    WRITELN('that you have lived, and the present position of ',
            'each cycle (leap');
    WRITELN('years are taken into account).');
    WRITELN;
    WRITELN;
    WRITELN('Enter all dates in month, day, year format ',
            '(for example: 10 23 1945).');
    WRITELN;
    WRITELN;
    WaitForAnyKey;
  END;


PROCEDURE PrintBior(A, B, C: REAL);

  VAR
    Tex: STRING [80];


  PROCEDURE PrintSet;

    VAR
      P, I, E: INTEGER;


    FUNCTION Line(A, B, C: INTEGER; D, E, F: CHAR): BOOLEAN;
      BEGIN
        IF (A < B) AND (A < C) THEN
          BEGIN
            Line := TRUE;
            INSERT(D, Tex, A);
            IF (B = C) THEN

              BEGIN
                INSERT('X', Tex, B);
                EXIT;
              END;
            IF (B < C) THEN

              BEGIN
                INSERT(E, Tex, B);
                INSERT(F, Tex, C);
              END
            ELSE

             BEGIN
               INSERT(F, Tex, C);
               INSERT(E, Tex, B);
             END;
           EXIT;
         END
       ELSE
         Line := FALSE;
     END;
```

Figure 5.3: (continued)

```
      BEGIN
        P := ROUND(A);
        I := ROUND(B);
        E := ROUND(C);

        IF Line(P, E, I, 'P', 'E', 'I') THEN EXIT;
        IF Line(E, P, I, 'E', 'P', 'I') THEN EXIT;
        IF Line(I, P, E, 'I', 'P', 'E') THEN EXIT;

        IF (P = E) AND (P < I) THEN
          BEGIN
            INSERT('X', Tex, P);
            INSERT('I', Tex, I);
            EXIT
          END;
        IF (P = I) AND (P < E) THEN
          BEGIN
            INSERT('X', Tex, P);
            INSERT('E', Tex, E);
            EXIT
          END;
        IF (E = I) AND (E < P) THEN
          BEGIN
            INSERT('X', Tex, E);
            INSERT('P', Tex, P);
            EXIT
          END;
        IF (P = I) AND (I = E) THEN
          INSERT('X', Tex, P);
        EXIT;
      END;

    BEGIN
      IF Month2 < 10 THEN WRITE(Out, Space);
      IF Day2 < 10 THEN WRITE(Out, Space);
      WRITE(Out, Month2, '/', Day2, '/', Year2);
      Tex := Dup(80, Space);
      Printset;
      WRITELN(Out, Copy(Tex, 9, 69));
    END;


PROCEDURE Display;

  VAR
    Index: INTEGER;


  PROCEDURE CalcBior(TotalDays: INTEGER;
                     VAR P, I, E: Real);
    BEGIN
      P := Pi * ((((TotalDays/23) - INT(TotalDays/23))*23)*(360/23))/180;
      E := Pi * ((((TotalDays/28) - INT(TotalDays/28))*28)*(360/28))/180;
      I := Pi * ((((TotalDays/33) - INT(TotalDays/33))*33)*(360/33))/180;
      P := INT(SIN(P) * 26 + 45.5);
      E := INT(SIN(E) * 26 + 45.5);
      I := INT(SIN(I) * 26 + 45.5);
    END;
```

Figure 5.3: (continued)

```
PROCEDURE NextDay(VAR Month, Day, Year: INTEGER; VAR Days: MonthArray);
  BEGIN
    INC(Day);
    IF Day > Days[Month] THEN
      BEGIN
        Day := 1;
        INC(Month);
      END;
    IF Month >= 13 THEN
      BEGIN
        Month := 1;
        INC(Year)
      END;
    IF INT(Year / 4) = Year / 4 THEN
      Days[2] := 29
    ELSE
      Days[2] := 28;
  END;

BEGIN
  IF Printout THEN
    WRITE(Out, CHR(12))
  ELSE
    CLRSCR;
  WRITELN(Out);
  WRITELN(Out, 'Biorhythm Chart for: ', Name);
  WRITELN(Out, 'Date of Birth: ', Months[Month1], ' ', Day1, ', ', Year1);
  WRITELN(Out, 'Starting Date: ', Months[Month2], ' ', Day2, ', ', Year2);
  WRITELN(Out);
  WRITELN(Out);
  WRITELN(Out, Dup(79, '-'));
  WRITELN(Out, '   Date', Space: 13, '-', Space: 25, '|', Space: 25, '+');
  WRITELN(Out, Dup(79, '-'));
  FOR Index := 1 TO LengthOfReport DO

    BEGIN
      CalcBior(TotalDays, Physical, Intellectual, Emotional);
      PrintBior(Physical, Intellectual, Emotional);
      NextDay(Month2, Day2, Year2, Days);
      Inc(TotalDays);
    END;
  END;


PROCEDURE Start;


  FUNCTION NumDays(M1, D1, Y1, M2, D2, Y2: INTEGER): INTEGER;

    VAR
      Year, DayCount: INTEGER;


    FUNCTION CalcDays(M, D: Integer): INTEGER;

      VAR
        I, J: INTEGER;
```

Figure 5.3: (continued)

```
        BEGIN
          J := 0;
          FOR I := M TO 12 DO
            J := J + Days[I];
          CalcDays := J - (D + 1);
        END;

      BEGIN
        DayCount := CalcDays(M1, D1)+((Y2-Y1)*365)-CalcDays(M2,D2);
        FOR Year := Y1 TO Y2 DO
          IF INT(Year / 4) = Year / 4 THEN
            INC(DayCount);
        NumDays := DayCount;
      END;

    BEGIN
      CLRSCR;
      WRITELN;
      WRITE('Enter your name: ');
      READLN(Name);
      WRITELN;
      WRITE('Enter your birthdate (mm dd yyyy): ');
      READLN(Month1, Day1, Year1);
      WRITELN;
      WRITE('Enter chart''s starting date (mm dd yyyy): ');
      READLN(Month2, Day2, Year2);
      IF Year1 < 100 THEN Year1 := Year1 + 1900;
      IF Year2 < 100 THEN Year2 := Year2 + 1900;
      WRITELN;
      WRITE('How many days do you want charted: ');

      READLN(LengthOfReport);
      Total_days := NumDays(Month1, Day1, Year1, Month2, Day2, Year2);
      WRITELN;
      WRITELN('Days from birth to start: ', TotalDays);
      WRITELN;

      Printout := YesOrNo('Do you want a printout of this chart?');
      IF Printout THEN
        ASSIGN(Out, 'LST:')
      ELSE
        ASSIGN(Out, 'CON:');
      Display;
    END;

  BEGIN
    Done := FALSE;
    REPEAT;
      Init;
      PrintHead;
      Start;
      WRITELN;
      WRITELN;
      WRITELN;
      IF NOT YesOrNo('Do you wish another chart?') THEN
        Done := TRUE;
    UNTIL Done;
  END.
```

Figure 5.3: (continued)

6 Operating-System Routines

Introduction

This chapter includes routines that can be used to access some of the many features of the MS-DOS/PC-DOS operating system. These routines include accessing the "command-line tail"—the series of parameters typed after the program name at the DOS prompt—as well as opening files, testing the printer status, and changing the border color of the screen (on a color display). Other examples were provided in the Date and Time routines in the first chapter. The program examples include a file-copy program, a listing program, a tab-expansion program, and a demonstration of the border color routine.

Opening Files—FILES.INC

The first routine provides a standard module to get arguments from the DOS command line and to open one or two files as named there—the first for input and the second for output. This function is designed for Turbo Pascal 3.0 and later versions, and takes advantage of the built-in PARAMCOUNT and PARAMSTR functions. Any remaining command-line parameters are available to the calling program by the use of these two functions.

Function *OpenFiles* is included in programs as

```
FILES.INC
```

It is called with two parameters—the number of files expected on the command line (1 or 2) and whether the routine should continue and return an error code or halt if an error is detected. The function returns a result code upon completion:

0 = Operation successful
1 = Input file open error
2 = Output file open error
3 = Duplicate file names
4 = Too few parameters on command line

The *OpenFiles* function checks the number of parameters entered on the command line and compares this value with the number of parameters expected. If the number is greater than or equal to that specified by the calling routine, the first file is opened using the first parameter string. If no error is encountered, if the number of parameters expected and entered was at least 2, and if the two file names are not the same, the output file is opened using the second parameter string. If the output file exists, the user is asked to confirm that it should be overwritten. A result code is returned when the function ends.

If an error is detected, function *Error* is called. It sets the result code if *Continue* has a Boolean value of TRUE or prints an error message with the error code and halts if *Continue* is FALSE.

```
FUNCTION OpenFiles(NumberExpected: INTEGER;
                   Continue: BOOLEAN): INTEGER;

 { This function will open one or two files specified in the DOS        }
 { command line: the first for input and the second for output,         }
 { based on the number of command line parameters expected.             }
 { Change the file types above as required for your program.            }
 { If successful, 0 is returned, otherwise an error code.               }
 {                                                                      }
 {                Result codes:                                         }
 {                0 = Operation successful;                             }
 {                1 = Input file open error;                            }
 {                2 = Output file open error;                           }
 {                3 = Duplicate file names;                             }
 {                4 = Too few parameters;                               }
 {                                                                      }
 { If you wish the program to continue and not halt on an file error,  }
 { set the Continue parameter to TRUE when calling the function.        }
 { This function requires ROUTINES.INC to be included before it.        }

  VAR
    Ok: BOOLEAN;
    Result: INTEGER;


  FUNCTION Error(Code: INTEGER): INTEGER;
    BEGIN
      IF Continue THEN
        Error := Code
      ELSE
        BEGIN
          WRITELN;
          WRITELN('File opening error #', Code, ' - halting.');
          HALT;
        END;
    END;

  BEGIN
    Result := 0;
    IF PARAMCOUNT >= NumberExpected THEN
      BEGIN
        ASSIGN(InputFile, PARAMSTR(1));
        {$I-}
        RESET(InputFile);
        {$I+}
        Ok := (IORESULT = 0);
        IF NOT Ok THEN
          BEGIN
            WRITELN('ERROR -- Input file ', UpString(PARAMSTR(1)),
                    ' not found.');
            Result := Error(1);
          END;
        IF (NumberExpected > 1) AND (PARAMCOUNT > 1) AND (Result = 0)
          THEN
          BEGIN
            IF UpString(PARAMSTR(1)) <> UpString(PARAMSTR(2))
              THEN
              BEGIN
                Assign(OutputFile, PARAMSTR(2));
```

Figure 6.1: The OpenFiles function in the include file FILES.INC.

```
                {$I-}
                Reset(OutputFile);
                {$I+}
                Ok := (IORESULT <> 0);
                IF NOT Ok THEN
                  BEGIN
                    WRITELN('ERROR -- Output file ',
                            'UpString(PARAMSTR(2)), exists.');
                    IF YesOrNo('Overwrite?') THEN
                      REWRITE(OutputFile)
                    ELSE
                      Result := Error(2);
                  END
                ELSE
                  REWRITE(OutputFile);
              END
            ELSE
              Result := Error(3);
          END;
    END
  ELSE
    Result := Error(4);
  OpenFiles := Result;
END;
```

Figure 6.1: (continued)

A File-Copy Program—FCOPY.PAS

The file-copy program is a good example of the use of the *OpenFiles* function. When compiled with Turbo 3.0 or later, *FCOPY.PAS*, listed in Figure 6.2, functions much like the DOS command COPY. The main difference is that *FCOPY* requires complete file names for both the source and destination files.

FCOPY uses Turbo Pascal's BLOCKREAD and BLOCKWRITE procedures for fast disk access. These functions use untyped files and copy the data directly to and from a buffer provided in the user program. They are very fast because no intermediate system buffer is used to hold the data temporarily. The block functions access multiples of 128 bytes of data at a time (one block). For the *FCOPY* program, I have provided a buffer array of 200 blocks of 128 bytes each to hold the data. This buffer size allows efficient use of the block disk-transfer capabilities of Turbo Pascal.

The *FCOPY* program first attempts to open the input and output files specified in the command line with the *OpenFiles* function discussed earlier. If this operation is successful, it begins copying and continues until all records are transferred or a write error is detected. The files are closed and the appropriate completion message is displayed.

The *FCOPY* program also illustrates how the block functions can be used to transfer data to and from the program very quickly—much faster than with the normal READ and WRITE procedures.

```
PROGRAM FileCopy;

  CONST
    RecSize = 128;
    BufSize = 200;

  VAR
    InputFile, OutputFile: FILE;       {untyped file for block operations}
    Buffer: ARRAY [1..RecSize, 1..BufSize] OF BYTE;
    RecsRead, Result: INTEGER;
    WriteErr: BOOLEAN;

    {$I ROUTINE.INC }
    {$I FILES.INC }

  BEGIN
    Result := OpenFiles(2, TRUE);
    IF Result = 0 THEN
      BEGIN
        WriteErr := FALSE;
        REPEAT
          BLOCKREAD(Input_File, Buffer, Bufsize, RecsRead);
          {$I-}
          BLOCKWRITE(Output_File, Buffer, RecsRead);
          {$I+}
          WriteErr := IORESULT <> 0;
        UNTIL (RecsRead = 0) OR WriteErr;
        CLOSE(InputFile);
        CLOSE(OutputFile);
        IF WriteErr THEN
          WRITELN('File copy error.')
        ELSE
          WRITELN('Copy successful.');
      END
    ELSE
      BEGIN
        WRITELN('Command line parameter error #', Result, '. ');
        WRITELN;
        WRITELN('Use: FCOPY d:SRCFILE.TYP d:DESTFILE.TYP  ');
      END;
  END.
```

Figure 6.2: The file-copy program FCOPY.PAS.

Printer Status Routines—PRINT.INC

The include file *PRINT.INC* (no pun intended) consists of two functions that allow you to test or reset the printer's status and to make sure the printer is ready before attempting a WRITE(LST, . . .) operation. As many programmers have found to their grief, if an output device is not ready when DOS attempts to use it, an error message is displayed on the screen, and the user can either try the device again or abort the program in progress. This is a poor solution to the problem; DOS's system-level error handling should be avoided if at all possible.

The *PrinterBIOS* function, listed in Figure 6.3, accesses the IBM PC BIOS service for the printer—interrupt 17 hex—either to reset the printer or to obtain its status. The function's parameters are the function number (1 or 2) requested and the printer number (1, 2, or 3) to use. It returns a bit-mapped 8-bit status word, which may be tested for six different printer conditions.

These conditions are:

Bit 7:	Not Busy	:=	status AND 128 > 0
Bit 6:	Acknowledge	:=	status AND 64 > 0
Bit 5:	OutofPaper	:=	status AND 32 > 0
Bit 4:	Selected	:=	status AND 16 > 0
Bit 3:	IOError	:=	status AND 8 > 0
Bit 0:	TimeOut	:=	status AND 1 > 0

Note that on some newer printers, IOError is used with Selected so that either may indicate a not-Selected condition. To be sure, you must test both conditions with a logical OR relation.

The *PrintTest* function, listed in Figure 6.4, makes extensive use of the *PrinterBIOS* function to ensure that the printer is on-line (selected) and ready to print before any output is sent to it. The only parameter to this function is the printer number to be tested (1, 2, or 3). It returns a Boolean TRUE if the printer is ready (or a problem detected earlier was corrected) and FALSE if the user elected to quit the print operation.

```
FUNCTION Printer_Bios(Func_Num: Integer;
                      Printer_Num: Integer): Integer;

{ This function accessed the printer BIOS routines using interrupt 17 hex.}
{ The DX register is set to zero for printer 1 or to 1 to for printer 2.  }
{ The AH register is set to indicate the BIOS function.  Function 1 is    }
{ used to hardware-reset the printer (and select it), and function 2 reads}
{ the printer status. After the interrupt, the printer status is in the   }
{ AH register.  The status word is decoded as follows:                    }
{                                                                         }
{ Bit #: 7     6     5     4     3   2 - 1   0                            }
{        |     |     |     |     |     |     |                            }
{        |     |     |     |     |     |     - 1 = Time-out               }
{        |     |     |     |     |     - Not used                         }
{        |     |     |     |     - 1 = I/O Error                          }
{        |     |     |     - 1 = Selected                                 }
{        |     |     - 1 = Out of Paper                                   }
{        |     - 1 = Acknowledge                                          }
{        - 1 = Not Busy                                                   }
{                                                                         }
{  The bit values can be tested by ANDing with integers as follows:       }
{                                                                         }
{            status := printer_Bios(2,1);                                 }
{                                                                         }
{  Bit 7:    Not busy    := status AND 128 > 0                            }
{  Bit 6:    Acknowledge  := status AND 64 > 0                            }
{  Bit 5:    OutOfPaper := status AND 32 > 0                              }
{  Bit 4:    Selected    := status AND 16 > 0                             }
{  Bit 3:    IOError     := status AND 8 > 0                              }
{  Bit 0:    TimeOut    := status AND 1 > 0                               }

 TYPE
   RegRec =
     RECORD
       Al, Ah, Bl, Bh, Cl, Ch: BYTE;
       Dx, Bp, Si, Di, Ds, Es, Flags: INTEGER;
     END;

 VAR
   Regs: RegRec;

 BEGIN
   WITH Regs DO
     BEGIN
       Ah := FuncNum; { Set AH to function number. }
       Dx := PrinterNum - 1; { Set DX to indicate which printer. }
       IF FuncNum = 1 THEN { Check for reset function }
         DELAY(1000); { Wait for prior functions to finish. }
       INTR($17, Regs); { Invoke interrupt 17 hex. }
       IF FuncNum = 1 THEN { Check for reset function }
         DELAY(2000); { Wait for the printer to finish resetting. }
       PrinterBios := Ah;
     END;

 END;
```

Figure 6.3: The PrinterBIOS function in the include file PRINT.INC.

```
FUNCTION PrintTest(PrinterNum: INTEGER): BOOLEAN;

  VAR
    PaperOut, OffLine, Quit: BOOLEAN;
    Status, Dummy: BYTE;
    Ch: CHAR;
  BEGIN
    Quit := FALSE;
    REPEAT
      Status := PrinterBios(2, PrinterNum);
      IF ((16 AND Status) = 0) OR ((8 AND Status) > 0) THEN
        BEGIN
          Dummy := PrinterBios(1, PrinterNum);
          Status := PrinterBios(2, PrinterNum);
        END;
      OffLine := ((16 AND Status) = 0) OR ((8 AND Status) > 0);
      PaperOut := (32 AND Status) > 0;
      IF OffLine THEN
        WRITELN('ERROR - Printer not on line.'^G);
      IF PaperOut THEN
        WRITELN('ERROR - Printer out of paper.'^G);
      IF OffLine OR PaperOut THEN
        BEGIN
          WRITELN;
          WRITE('Correct problem and press ENTER or "Q" to quit: ');
          Read(KBD, Ch);
          IF UPCASE(Ch) = 'Q' THEN
            Quit := TRUE;
          WRITELN;
          WRITELN;
        END;
    UNTIL (NOT OffLine AND NOT PaperOut) OR Quit;
    PrintTest := NOT Quit;
  END;
```

Figure 6.4: The PrintText function in the include file PRINT.INC.

A Listing Program—LIST.PAS

The program *LIST.PAS*, shown in Figure 6.5, will list a file to the printer with page formatting. It also allows the user to select the print mode (Emphasized, Condensed, or Regular) on Epson-compatible printers. The listing includes the date and time of the printout, the file name, and the page number. The program also supports path names and drive identifiers (when used with Turbo Pascal 3.0). It requires three include files—*ROUTINE.INC*, *FILES .INC*, and *PRINT.INC*.

The program begins by opening the input file specified in the command line or by the user. The printer status is tested, and the system date and time are saved in variables (remember that the system time is constantly changing) so that they will be the same on each page of the listing. The file is read and printed line by line. A form-feed and page heading are output every 55 lines. The program terminates when an EOF condition is detected.

```
PROGRAM List;

 { This program is a file lister.  The file name may be put on the     }
 { command line, but if it is not the program will                     }
 { prompt the user for the file name.                                  }
 { Examples:                                                           }
 {          list list.pas   list c:/tpas/list.pas  or just  list       }
 {                                                                     }
 { If the file name is not specified on the command line, the program }
 { will also let the user change an Epson printer's setup to give      }
 { either compressed or emphasized type.                               }

 CONST
   MaxLines = 55;
   Formfeed = ^L;
   Space = ' ';

   {$I ROUTINE.INC }

 TYPE
   Linetype = UniversalString;
   Filename_Str = STRING [24];

 VAR
   Linecount, Page, Result: INTEGER;
   Infile: FilenameStr;
   Date1, Time1, Line: Linetype;
   InputFile, OutputFile: TEXT;      {OutputFile required for FILES.INC}
   Ok, ManualEntry: BOOLEAN;

   {$I FILES.INC }


 PROCEDURE Printer;

   CONST
     Emph = ^['E';
     Comp = ^O;
     Reset = ^['@';
     Tof = ^L;

   VAR
     Command: CHAR;
     Quit: BOOLEAN;
     I: INTEGER;

   BEGIN
     Quit := FALSE;
     CLRSCR;
     FOR I := 1 TO 8 DO
     WRITELN;
     WRITELN(Space: 15, 'Epson printer modes:');
     WRITELN;
     WRITELN(Space: 15, 'E -- Emphasized');
     WRITELN(Space: 15, 'C -- Compress');
     WRITELN(Space: 15, 'R -- Reset codes');
     WRITELN(Space: 15, 'T -- Top of Form');
     WRITELN(Space: 15, 'Q -- Quit');
```

Figure 6.5: The file-listing program LIST.PAS.

```
    WRITELN;
    WRITE('Enter command: ');
    WHILE NOT Quit DO
      BEGIN
        REPEAT
          READ(KBD, Command);
          Command := UPCASE(Command);
        UNTIL Command IN ['E', 'C', 'R', 'T', 'Q'];
        WRITE(Command);
        CASE Command OF
          'E': WRITE(LST, Emph);
          'C': WRITE(LST, Comp);
          'R': WRITE(LST, Reset);
          'T': WRITE(LST, Tof);
          'Q': Quit := TRUE
          END; { end case }
      END; { end while }
    CLRSCR;
  END; { end printer }

{$I PRINT.INC }


PROCEDURE PrintHeader(Page: INTEGER;
                      InFileName: FilenameStr);
  BEGIN
    WRITE(LST, Formfeed);
    WRITELN(LST);
    WRITE(LST, '    ', InFileName);
    WRITE(LST, Space: 55);
    WRITELN(LST, 'Page #', Page: 3);
    WRITELN;
    WRITE(LST, '    ', Date1);
    WRITELN(LST, Space: 47, Time1);
    WRITELN(LST);
    WRITELN(LST);
  END;

BEGIN { Start main program }
  WRITELN('File list program for Epson and IBM printers.');
  WRITELN;
  ManualEntry := FALSE;
  Result := OpenFiles(1, TRUE);   { OpenFiles is in FILES.INC }
  IF Result <> 0 THEN
    BEGIN
      ManualEntry := TRUE;
      REPEAT
        WRITE('Enter file name to list (Paths OK): ');
        READLN(Infile);
        ASSIGN(InputFile, Infile);
        {$I-}
        RESET(InputFile);
        {$I+}
        Ok := (IORESULT = 0);
        IF NOT Ok THEN
          WRITELN('ERROR -- Input file ', UpString(Infile),
                  ' not found.');
      UNTIL Ok;
    END
```

Figure 6.5: (continued)

```
    ELSE
      Infile := PARAMSTR(1);
    IF PrintTest(1) THEN                {Print_Test is in PRINT.INC }
      BEGIN
        IF ManualEntry THEN
          IF Yesorno('Set Printer mode?') THEN
            Printer;
        Time1 := Time;
        Date1 := Date;
        WRITELN('Printing ', UpString(Infile));
        Page := 1;
        Linecount := 0;
        WRITE(LST, '    ', Date1);
        WRITELN(LST, Space: 47, Time1);
        WRITELN(LST);
        WRITELN(LST, Space: 30, Upstring(Infile));
        WRITELN(LST);
        WRITELN(LST);
        WHILE NOT EOF(InputFile) DO
          BEGIN
            READLN(InputFile, Line);
            INC(Linecount);
            IF Linecount >= MaxLines THEN
              BEGIN
                INC(Page);
                PrintHeader(Page, UpString(Infile));
                Linecount := 0;
              END;
            WRITELN(LST, '       ', Line);
          END;
        CLOSE(InputFile);
        WRITE(LST, Formfeed);
      END
    ELSE
      WRITELN('Program terminated.');
  END.
```

Figure 6.5: (continued)

A Tab-Conversion Program—EXPTABS.PAS

The Turbo editor does not use tab characters for screen formatting, although it does display them (and other control characters) in low-intensity mode on the screen. If you are attempting to work with a program originally written using tabs, it is a tedious job to edit the program for Turbo by expanding each tab character to the right number of spaces.

The program *EXPTABS.PAS*, listed in Figure 6.6, will perform this job quickly and effortlessly. It uses the include files *ROUTINE .INC* and *FILES.INC*. Unlike the modified *FILTER.PAS* program presented in Chapter 2, this program maintains the intended program format exactly, by substituting the correct number of spaces for each tab character encountered in the text.

Like the *LIST* program, *EXPTABS* uses command-line parameters. The input file name, output file name, and optional tab spacing value are the expected parameters. Path names and drive identifiers can also be included.

The procedure *Process* converts the text file, reading one line at a time, checking for tabs, converting them to spaces, and writing the modified line to the output file. The technique for tab conversion is a little tricky in that a tab may appear anywhere in a line, but tab stops are at fixed intervals, as on a typewriter. Therefore, each time a tab is detected, the number of spaces to the next tab stop must be calculated.

If incorrect parameters or no parameters are entered on the command line, the program provides an error message and usage examples.

```
PROGRAM Exptabs;

  CONST
    DefaultSpaces = 8;
    Space = ' ';
    Tab = #9;

    {$I ROUTINE.INC }

  VAR
    Line, NewLine: UniversalString;
    Result, LinePos, Count, Err, NextChar, NumSpaces: INTEGER;
    InputFile, OutputFile: TEXT;

    {$I FILES.INC }


  PROCEDURE Process;
    BEGIN
      IF PARAMCOUNT = 3 THEN
        BEGIN
          VAL(PARAMSTR(3), NumSpaces, Err);
          IF Err <> 0 THEN
            NumSpaces := DefaultSpaces;
        END
      ELSE
        NumSpaces := DefaultSpaces;
      WHILE NOT EOF(InputFile) DO
        BEGIN
          READLN(InputFile, Line);
          NewLine := '';
          NextChar := 1;
          FOR LinePos := 1 TO LENGTH(Line) DO
            BEGIN
              IF Line[LinePos] = Tab THEN
                BEGIN
                  REPEAT
                    NewLine := NewLine + Space;
                    INC(NextChar);
                  UNTIL (NextChar > NumSpaces) AND
                        ((NextChar MOD NumSpaces) = 1);
                END
              ELSE
                BEGIN
                  NewLine := NewLine + Line[LinePos];
                  INC(NextChar);
                END;
            END;
          WRITELN(OutputFile, NewLine);
        END;
      CLOSE(InputFile);
      CLOSE(OutputFile);
      WRITELN('Conversion completed.');
    END;
```

Figure 6.6: The tab-conversion program EXPTABS.PAS.

```
BEGIN
  WRITELN('EXPTABS - Expands tabs to spaces in text file.');
  WRITELN;
  Result := OpenFiles(2, TRUE);
  IF Result = 0 THEN
    Process
  ELSE
    BEGIN
      WRITELN;
      WRITELN('Command line parameter error #', Result, '.');
      WRITELN;
      WRITELN('Usage:');
      WRITELN('     EXPTABS <input filename> <output filename> ',
              '[<# spaces, default 8>]');
      WRITELN('Examples:');
      WRITELN('     EXPTABS OLD.TXT NEW.TXT ');
      WRITELN('     EXPTABS OLD.TXT NEW.TXT 6');
    END;
END.
```

Figure 6.6: (continued)

Setting the Screen Border Color—SETBDR.PAS

Turbo Pascal 3.0 provides built-in routines for setting the text foreground and background colors. However, if you also want to choose the screen border color, you must provide your own routine.

The simple procedure provided in *SETBDR.PAS,* listed in Figure 6.7, will work on most IBM PCs and compatibles. It has the advantage of being very short and simple, and the disadvantage of being hardware-specific. It outputs a value directly to the CRT display chip on the Color/Graphics Adapter card to set the border color. If your programs must run on other types of machines, the more complex BIOS CRT interrupt 10 hex should be used instead.

The procedure *SetBorder* has one parameter, an integer between 0 and 15 specifying the color to use for the border. You may also use the predefined color constants in Turbo 3.0, listed on pages 308–9 of the *Turbo Pascal 3.0 Reference Manual* (Borland International, 1985) to select the color.

The demonstration program will cycle through all available colors at intervals of about one second. It will stop at the end of a cycle if any key is pressed.

```
PROGRAM BorderColors;

  VAR
    I: INTEGER;


  PROCEDURE SetBorder(Color: BYTE);

    BEGIN
      Port[$03D9] := $F AND Color;    { Direct output to color card chip }
    END;

  BEGIN
    REPEAT
      FOR I := 0 TO 15 DO
        BEGIN
          SetBorder(I);
          DELAY(1000);
        END;
    UNTIL Keypressed;
    SetBorder(0);
  END.
```

Figure 6.7: The program SETBDR.PAS to set the border color.

7 Business Programs

Introduction

By this point, the advantages of creating a library of building blocks and specialized include files should be clear. Similarly, it should be obvious that breaking programming tasks into clearly defined, self-documenting modules is critical to using Turbo most effectively and writing programs efficiently.

The programs in this chapter deal with several small real-world applications of Turbo programming. One of the problems in writing about Turbo Pascal is trying to show that it is capable of tackling truly ambitious projects. The language is particularly well-suited for programs running between 1000 and 5000 lines of code, and it is perfectly capable of dealing with programs in excess of 50,000 lines. Of course, it is impractical to put a program of that size in a book such as this. On the other hand, by using much shorter programs one runs the risk of presenting Turbo as a language suitable only for trivial problems.

Although the format of this book does not allow for a really long program, I hope that the simple programs in this chapter demonstrate that Turbo—even in tackling modest tasks—really does lend itself to real-world applications. The programs presented in this chapter illustrate how a library of routines and include files can be combined and modified quickly to address some typical real-world applications. In all cases it makes obvious practical sense to use the power and convenience of the personal computer to do some repetitive day-to-day calculations.

Converting Metric to Printer's Units—METRIC.PAS

The program called *METRIC.PAS*, in Figure 7.1, illustrates how easy it is to write a custom application once you have assembled even a small toolbox of programming routines. The application is obviously a specialized one, and I am certain that you will not find a millimeters-to-picas conversion program on any bulletin board. That does not mean that a one-of-a-kind program like this had to be a major development effort. And it certainly was worth the small programming effort that was required, in light of the frequency with which I have to do precise (rather than approximate) conversions. I am sure that you are already seeing your own job-specific parallels with this program.

The program uses three of the four major include files—*TITLE.INC*, *WINDOWS.INC* and *ROUTINE.INC*. It also includes, as a comment, a list of the constants used to remind me (when I get around to it) that there is room to improve the accuracy of the program even futher.

Putting the program together was a simple matter of creating an attractive screen and writing three new routines—*EnglishInput*, *MetricInput*, and *PrinterInput*—to do the actual calculations.

There are twelve points in a pica. Type sizes are given in points (never picas and points), but linear measurements are always given in picas and points. Hence the need for a printout of *TotalPoints* as well as the MOD/DIV/TRUNC routines to display picas and points simultaneously. Even this archaic, nondecimal measuring system did not cause any programming hassles.

```
PROGRAM MetricConverter;
{$I Windows.inc}
{$I Title.inc}
{$I Routine.inc}
{Note: 1 mm = 2.85 points
      25.4 mm = 72.points
      1.00 picas = 4.23 mm
       mm to inch: .04
       in to mm: 25.4
       mm to pica: .236
       pica to mm: 4.23
       mm to point: 2.85
       point to mm: .3515
       }

CONST
  MetricWindow   : Corners = (4,8,19,13);
  EnglishWindow : Corners = (28,8,43,13);
  PrinterWindow  : Corners = (52,8,76,13);
  UserDialog     : Corners = (4,16,76,20);
  Normal         : Corners = (1,1,80,24);
VAR
  Picas, TotalPoints, Points, MUnits, EUnits, PUnits,  InUnits : REAL;
  Scheme : CHAR;

PROCEDURE ScreenSetUp;
BEGIN
  TEXTCOLOR (4);
  DoWindow (Normal);  {garbage collection}
  CLRSCR;
  GOTOXY (3,4);
  WRITELN ('CONVERSION CALCULATOR BETWEEN METRIC, ENGLISH, AND PRINTER''S
           MEASUREMENTS');
  GOTOXY (9,6);
  WRITELN ('METRIC');
  MakeFrame (MetricWindow,#205, #186);
  GOTOXY (32,6);
  WRITELN ('ENGLISH');
  MakeFrame (EnglishWindow,#205, #186);
  GOTOXY (59,6);
  WRITELN ('PRINTER');
  MakeFrame (PrinterWindow,#205, #186);
  TEXTCOLOR (4);
END;

PROCEDURE Display;
BEGIN
  TEXTCOLOR (0);  {Black letters}
  DoWindow (MetricWindow);
  GOTOXY (3,3);
  WRITE (MUnits:5:2);
  WRITELN (' mm');
  DoWindow (EnglishWindow);
  GOTOXY (3,3);
  WRITE (EUnits:5:2);
  WRITELN (' inch');
```

Figure 7.1: The program METRIC.PAS to convert between metric, English, and printer's measurements. It demonstrates the combination of standard routines to solve an ad hoc programming task.

```
  DoWindow (PrinterWindow);
  GOTOXY (3,2);
  WRITELN (Picas:5:2, ' Pica ', Points:5:2, ' pt');
  GOTOXY (5,5);
  WRITELN (TotalPoints:5:2,' Points');
  DoWindow (Normal);
  TEXTCOLOR (4); {Back to red}
END;

PROCEDURE MetricInput;
BEGIN
  MUnits := InUnits;
  EUnits := MUnits * (0.03934);
  TotalPoints := MUnits * 2.85;
  Picas := MUnits * 0.236 ;
  Points := (TRUNC (TotalPoints)) MOD 12;
END;

PROCEDURE EnglishInput;
VAR
  PicaInt, PointInt : INTEGER;
BEGIN
  EUnits := InUnits;
  MUnits := EUnits * (25.4);
  TotalPoints := EUnits * 72;
  PicaInt := (TRUNC (TotalPoints)) DIV 12;
  PointInt := (TRUNC (TotalPoints)) MOD 12;
  Picas := PicaInt;
  Points := PointInt;
END;


PROCEDURE PrinterInput;
BEGIN
  Picas := InUnits;
  TotalPoints := (Picas * 12) + Points;
  EUnits := TotalPoints / 72;
  MUnits := TotalPoints * 0.3515;
END;

PROCEDURE InitializeEverything;
BEGIN
  TEXTBACKGROUND (3);  {Light blue background}
  TEXTCOLOR (4);  {Red letters}
  CLRSCR;
  PrintMessage ('UNIVERSAL',1);
  PrintMessage ('CONVERSION',9);
  PrintMessage ('PROGRAM',17);
  GOTOXY (22,24);
  WaitForAnyKey;
  CLRSCR;
  ScreenSetUp;
  DoWindow (Normal);
  GOTOXY (15,23);
  WRITELN ('TYPE -1 AND CARRIAGE RETURN TO QUIT');
END;
```

Figure 7.1: (continued)

```
PROCEDURE GetAndProcessUserInput;
BEGIN
  MakeFrame (UserDialog,#205,#186);
  DoWindow (UserDialog);
  CLRSCR;
  InUnits := 0;
  GOTOXY (9,2);
  WRITELN ('Remember space between picas and points: 18 9)');
  GOTOXY (4,3);
  WRITE ('WHAT IS THE INPUT VALUE [ MM / Inch / Picas Points]? ');
  TEXTCOLOR (0);
  GOTOXY (57,3);
  READLN (InUnits, Points);
  GOTOXY (7,4);
  TEXTCOLOR (4);
  WRITE ('IS IT METRIC, ENGLISH, OR PICAS/POINTS [M - E - P]? ');
  READ (KBD, Scheme);
  Scheme := UPCASE (Scheme);
  CASE Scheme OF
     'M' : MetricInput;
     'E' : EnglishInput;
     'P' : PrinterInput;
  END;
    Display;
END;


BEGIN
  InitializeEverything;
  REPEAT  GetAndProcessUserInput
    UNTIL  (InUnits = -1);
  DoWindow (Normal);
  CLRSCR;
END.
```

Figure 7.1: (continued)

Mortgage Amortization—MORTGAGE.PAS

The program *MORTGAGE.PAS* in Figure 7.2 is included for several reasons. First, it is fast and works quite nicely. Second, it also makes use of library routines. Third, because every collection of programs seems to have a mortgage program, it should prove instructive to compare this with versions written in other languages. Finally, it shows a simple arrangement for redirecting output from the screen to the line printer—a useful addition to almost any calculation routine.

Surprisingly, the financial calculations are the easiest and smallest part of this program. Most of the code is devoted to formatting the line printer output, doing the screen "window dressing," and providing clear user prompts to make the program easy to use. The program is still far from polished, but it does illustrate that a useful and user-friendly program can be assembled easily and in stages. The *FunctionSelection* variable, for example, can be modified to take on an additional range of values rather than the simple two-choice option used here.

```
PROGRAM Mortgage;
{$I title.inc}

VAR FunctionSelection, i: INTEGER;
    Payment, InterestRate, LoanAmount, Term1, Term2, Denominator: REAL;
    Rate, Periods, Numerator: REAL;
    ch: CHAR;

PROCEDURE Spacer(Number:INTEGER);
BEGIN
  FOR i := 1 TO Number DO
    WRITELN ;
END;

PROCEDURE WaitForAnyKey;        {Pauses and waits for any key.}
VAR
  AnyKey : CHAR;
BEGIN
  WRITELN ('To continue, please strike any key.');
  READ (KBD, AnyKey);
END;

PROCEDURE ScreenHeading;
BEGIN
  WRITELN;
  WRITELN ('      PRINCIPAL  MONTHLY   MONTHLY   PRINCIPAL INTEREST',
           '    YTD     MO YR');

  WRITELN (' PMT  BALANCE  PRINCIPAL  INTEREST   TO DATE   TO DATE   ',
           'INTEREST');
  WRITELN
END;

PROCEDURE NextScreen;
BEGIN
  WaitForAnyKey;
  CLRSCR;
  ScreenHeading
END;

PROCEDURE PaymentComp;
BEGIN
  REPEAT
    CLRSCR;
    WRITELN ('MORTGAGE COMPUTATION');
    WRITELN ('Enter the loan amount (assumes thousands), number of years,
 and interest rate');
    WRITELN ('For example $66,000 for 30 years at 12.5% interest
 would be - 66 30 12.5');
    WRITELN; READLN (LoanAmount, Periods, InterestRate);
    Periods := Periods * 12;
    LoanAmount := LoanAmount * 1000.0;
    Rate := InterestRate / 1200.0;
    Term1 := 1 + Rate;
    Term2 := EXP(-Periods * LN(Term1));
    Denominator := 1 - Term2;
    Payment := (Rate / Denominator) * LoanAmount;
```

Figure 7.2: The program MORTGAGE.PAS both calculates a mortgage repayment schedule and directs it to a line printer.

```
    CLRSCR;
    WRITELN ('          Interest rate       =  ',InterestRate:11:2,'%');
    WRITELN ('          Loan amount         = $',LoanAmount:11:2);
    WRITELN ('          Number of payments  = ',Periods:9:0);
    WRITELN;
    WRITELN ('          Payment amount will be $',Payment:8:2,
                        ' per period.');
    WRITELN ('          Repeat? [Y / N]');
    READ (KBD, ch);
  UNTIL UPCASE(ch) = 'N'
END; {PaymentComp}


PROCEDURE PaymentSchedule;
VAR
  BeginYear, BeginMonth, I          : INTEGER;
  Totalpay, Pay, Tpay, Mint, Mprin: REAL;
  Ytdi, Ytdp, Tmint, Tprin          : REAL;
  YesPrinter                        :BOOLEAN;
  PrintCounter,DisplayLines         :INTEGER;
  BlankString                       :STRING[20];


PROCEDURE GetParameters;
BEGIN
  WRITELN ('PAYMENT SCHEDULE COMPUTATION'); Spacer(3);
  WRITELN ('Enter the loan amount (assumes thousands), number of years,
and interest rate');
  WRITELN ('For example $66,000 for 30 years at 12.5% interest
would be - 66 30 12.5');
  WRITELN;
  READLN (LoanAmount, Periods, InterestRate);
  WRITELN;
  WRITELN ('Enter starting Month and Year: ');
  WRITELN ('Ex: 12 1984');
  READLN    ( BeginMonth , BeginYear);
  WRITELN;
  WRITELN ('How many payments would you like to see?');
  WRITELN (' ');
  READLN  (DisplayLines);
  WRITELN ('Send output to printer or screen ?  [P / S]');
  READ (KBD, ch);
  CLRSCR;
  IF UPCASE(ch) = 'P' THEN YesPrinter := TRUE
    ELSE YesPrinter := FALSE
END;


PROCEDURE PrinterHeading (VAR PrintCounter:INTEGER);
BEGIN
  WRITELN(LST);
  WRITELN(LST,'      PRINCIPAL  MONTHLY   MONTHLY   PRINCIPAL',
  ' INTEREST     YTD      MO YR');
  WRITELN(LST,' PMT  BALANCE  PRINCIPAL  INTEREST   TO DATE ',
  ' TO DATE    INTEREST');
  WRITELN;
  PrintCounter:= 0
END;
```

Figure 7.2: (continued)

```
PROCEDURE Spacer(Number:INTEGER);
BEGIN
  FOR i:= 1 TO Number DO
    WRITELN(LST,'      ')
END;


PROCEDURE Calculate;
BEGIN
  Tmint:=0.0;Ytdi:=0.0;Ytdp:=0.0;Tprin:=0.0;
  BlankString :='                      ';
  LoanAmount := LoanAmount * 1000;
  Periods := Periods * 12;
  Rate:= InterestRate / 1200.;
  Pay :=EXP( Periods * LN(1. + Rate));
  Pay := Rate * Pay / (Pay-1);
  Payment := Pay * LoanAmount;
  TotalPay := Payment * Periods;
  IF YesPrinter THEN BEGIN
    WRITELN ('Sending report to printer.....');
    Spacer(2);
    WRITELN (LST,BlankString,'        LOANER PRINTOUT');
    Spacer(2);
    WRITELN (LST,BlankString,'Interest :         ',InterestRate:11:2);
    Spacer(1);
    WRITELN (LST,BlankString,'Principal :        ',LoanAmount:11:2);
    Spacer(1);
    WRITELN (LST,BlankString,'Total Months:           ',Periods:4:0);
    Spacer(1);
    WRITELN (LST,BlankString,'Monthly Payment:   ',Payment:11:2);
    Spacer(1);
    WRITELN (LST,BlankString,'Total Amount:      ',TotalPay:11:2);
    PrinterHeading(PrintCounter)
  END

  ELSE
  BEGIN {screen display}
    (*
    WRITELN ('Interest rate                 ',InterestRate:11:2);
    WRITELN ('Number of payments                ',Periods:4:0);
    WRITELN ('Loan amount                   ',LoanAmount:11:2);
    WRITELN ('Monthly Payment               ',Payment:11:2);
    WRITELN ('Total Amount of all Payments  ',TotalPay:11:2);
    *)

    ScreenHeading
  END;

  FOR I:= 1 TO DisplayLines DO
    BEGIN
      Pay := EXP(I * LN (1. + rate));
      Pay := Rate * Pay / (Pay - 1);
      Tpay := Pay * I;
      Mint := LoanAmount * Rate;
      Mprin := Payment - Mint;
      Tprin := Tprin + Mprin;
      Tmint := Tmint + Mint;
```

Figure 7.2: (continued)

```
      LoanAmount := LoanAmount - Mprin;
      IF LoanAmount < 0 THEN LoanAmount := 0;
      Ytdp := Ytdp + Mprin;
      Ytdi := Ytdi + Mint;

    IF YesPrinter THEN
    BEGIN
      WRITE (LST, I:3, LoanAmount:10:2, mprin:10:2);
      WRITELN (LST,Mint:10:2,Tprin:10:2,Tmint:10:2,Ytdi:10:2,
BeginMonth:3,' ',BeginYear:2) ;
      PrintCounter:= PrintCounter + 1;
      IF PrintCounter = 50 THEN PrinterHeading(PrintCounter)
    END
    ELSE
      BEGIN
        WRITE (I:3, LoanAmount:10:2, Mprin:10:2, Mint:10:2, Tprin:10:2);
        WRITELN (Tmint:10:2, Ytdi:10:2, BeginMonth:3, ' ', BeginYear:2);
        BeginMonth := BeginMonth+1;
        PrintCounter:= PrintCounter + 1;
        IF ((PrintCounter MOD 18) = 0) THEN NextScreen;
        IF BeginMonth = 13 THEN
          BEGIN
            BeginYear := BeginYear +1;
          IF BeginYear = 100 THEN BeginYear := 0;
            Ytdp := 0;
            Ytdi := 0;
            BeginMonth := 1
        END {IF}
      END {IF}
  END; {IF/THEN/ELSE}
BEGIN
  REPEAT
    CLRSCR;
    GetParameters;
    Calculate;
    WRITELN (' Another go at it? [Y / N]');
    READ (KBD, ch);
  UNTIL UPCASE(ch) = 'N';
END; {PaymentSchedule}


PROCEDURE Setup; {Reads selection of function from keyboard.}
BEGIN
  CLRSCR;
  PrintMessage ('MORTGAGE',5);
  PrintMessage ('PROGRAM',14);
  GOTOXY (22,24);
  WaitForAnyKey;
  CLRSCR;
  WRITELN ('Select the number for the function you want:');
  WRITELN; WRITELN; WRITELN;
  WRITELN ('1.  PAYMENT, given interest rate, periods, loan amount.');
  WRITELN;
  WRITELN ('2.  PAYMENT AND SCHEDULE OF PAYMENTS with printer option.');
  WRITELN;
  REPEAT
    READ (KBD, ch);
    FunctionSelection := ORD (ch)-48;
```

Figure 7.2: (continued)

```
    CASE FunctionSelection OF
    1: PaymentComp;
    2: PaymentSchedule;
    ELSE FunctionSelection := 0;
    WRITELN ('Try again.');
    END; {case of FunctionSelection}
  UNTIL FunctionSelection <> 0
END; {Setup}



BEGIN {MainLine}
  Setup
END.
```

Figure 7.2: (continued)

Compound Interest—COMINT.PAS

The program *COMINT.PAS* in Figure 7.3 calculates compound interest. It is included just to emphasize that a common business application can be addressed with elegant display and user friendliness in a matter of minutes. Yet despite its simplicity, a program like this is among the most useful that we write because, ultimately, most of us have to do currency conversion, interest figuring, and loan calculations more often than we ever have to write mammoth communication programs from scratch.

The chapter concludes with a set of date-manipulation routines and some added screen I/O routines.

```
PROGRAM DemonstrateFunctionToComputeContinuallyCompoundedInterest;
{$I title.inc}
{$I routine.inc}
VAR
  Principal, Years, Rate, Amount : REAL;
  Iterations : INTEGER;
(*
TYPE
  UniversalString  = STRING [255];
VAR
  Phrase : UniversalString;


FUNCTION YesOrNo (PromptMessage : UniversalString) : BOOLEAN;
VAR
  Response : CHAR;
BEGIN
  WRITE(PromptMessage,' (Y/N) ');
  REPEAT
    READ (KBD, Response);
  UNTIL Response IN ['Y','y','N','n'];
  WRITE (Response);
  YesOrNo := Response IN ['Y','y'];
END;
*)
FUNCTION Interest (Principal, Term, Rate : REAL) : REAL;
VAR
  OneYearMultiplier, MultiYearMultiplier, PercentInterest : REAL;
BEGIN
  PercentInterest := Rate / 100.0;
  OneYearMultiplier := PercentInterest + 1.0;
  MultiYearMultiplier := EXP (Term * PercentInterest);
  Interest := Principal * MultiYearMultiplier;
END;   {Interest}


PROCEDURE DoInterest;
BEGIN
  CLRSCR;
  WRITELN ('Principal amount? (e.g. 30000 ) ');
  READLN (Principal);
  WRITELN ('Term in years?');
  READLN (Years);
  WRITELN ('Interest rate? (5 1/2 % would be 5.5) ');
  READLN (Rate);
  WRITELN ('The result is:');
  WRITELN (Interest (Principal, Years, Rate):6:2)
END;


BEGIN
  CLRSCR;
  PrintMessage ('FIGURE',1);
  PrintMessage ('COMPOUND',9);
  PrintMessage ('INTEREST',17);
  GOTOXY (22,24);
  WaitForAnyKey;
  DoInterest;
  WHILE (YesOrNo ('Do it again?')) DO DoInterest
END.
```

Figure 7.3: The program COMINT.PAS to calculate compound interest.

Date Routines—DATE.INC and DATETEST.PAS

When writing business-oriented programs it is often necessary to work with dates. They must be input, output, converted, added to or subtracted from, and so on. The routines in the include file *DATE.INC* provide most of the operations you might need to use, including string-to-integer conversion and integer-to-string conversion of dates, calendar date to modified Julian date, Julian date to calendar date, and day-of-the-week calculation. Also included are the constant arrays most often used in date operations.

Converting Dates between String and Integer

One of the most common date tasks is user input of a date. The easiest way this can be handled in Pascal is to ask the user to enter three integers for month, day, and year, and then use the statement

```
READLN(Month,Day,Year);
```

to get the data. This method works, but it is not user friendly and is most unforgiving of entry errors—any nonnumeric characters will cause the program to terminate. A more professional approach requires a little programming work but is well worth the effort.

First, a string is used to accept the input data, thus eliminating Turbo's data checking. Since this routine should be versatile, it must allow any nonnumeric character to be used as a data separator (between the month, day, and year data).

To pick out the valid data, a simple numeric parser is used in the routine *ParseDate*. It reads the input string until it finds numeric characters, then it converts the numeric characters to a number (in the variable *Num*) and returns when it encounters a nonnumeric character.

Procedure *DateToInt* uses function *ParseDate* to convert the input string to three integer values for the month, day, and year. For general compatibility, 1900 is added to the year value to obtain the actual year.

This routine allows the date to be entered in many different formats and still be acceptable:

MM/DD/YY
MM DD YY
MM-DD-YY
MM,DD,YY

The *IntToDate* function provides the reverse conversion from three integer values to a date string—a much simpler process. It uses Turbo's STR function to convert integer values to their string equivalents. These three short strings are concatenated with the symbol / to produce the traditional date format. A FOR loop converts spaces to zeros for a more consistent output. The function returns a string containing the formatted date.

Calendar and Julian Dates

Calculating with dates can be a real headache, but the process can be simplified by using modified "Julian" dates instead of the familiar calendar date. Julian dates were invented in 1582 as a "universal" method of calculating large time intervals. Each day in the valid time period has its own unique day number, and so the interval between any two dates can be easily calculated by addition or subtraction of their Julian numbers.

The formal Julian system starts counting with day one on January 1, 4713 B.C. and continues through A.D. 3267. For example, the standard Julian day number for January 1, 1962 was 2,437,665. To avoid using such large numbers, with their inherent accuracy problems, I have provided a modified Julian date routine that is valid (at least) from day 1 (January 1, 0001 A.D.) through day 999999 (November 6, 2738 A.D.). To convert from standard Julian dates to our modified form, simply add 1,721,409 to the modified Julian number.

Julian numbers are useful in financial, accounting, and calendar programs, which must determine the exact number of days between two dates.

Day of the Week

The final date routine, called *DayOfWeek*, calculates the correct day of the week for any date using Zeller's Congruence algorithm. Given the date in three integer variables, it returns an integer between 0 and 6 representing the day of the week. The returned value translates as follows (*DayArray* may be used to return a string containing the correct day name if the returned *DayOfWeek* value is used as an index):

0 = Sunday
1 = Monday
2 = Tuesday
3 = Wednesday
4 = Thursday
5 = Friday
6 = Saturday

Date Routine Test Program

The next program, listed in Figure 7.5, is used to demonstrate and test the operation of the date routine library. It requests a date string from the user, displays it in normal English format (January 1, 1986), determines what day of the week that date falls on, and displays the integer and Julian date values. Finally, it converts the calculated Julian date back to calendar date and prints it as a string.

```
CONST
  DayArray: ARRAY [0..6] OF STRING [9] =
  ('Sunday', 'Monday', 'Tuesday', 'Wednesday', 'Thursday', 'Friday',
   'Saturday');
  MonthArray: ARRAY [1..12] OF STRING [9] =
  ('January', 'February', 'March', 'April', 'May', 'June', 'July',
   'August', 'September', 'October', 'November', 'December');
  MonthDays: ARRAY [1..12] OF INTEGER =
  (31, 28, 31, 30, 31, 30, 31, 31, 30, 31, 30, 31);


TYPE
  Datestr = STRING [8];


PROCEDURE DateToInt(Date: Datestr; VAR Month, Day, Year: Integer);
{Converts a date string in the form MM/DD/YY to integer month, }
{day, and year}

VAR
  Position: INTEGER;


FUNCTION ParseDate(VAR I: INTEGER; Dat: Datestr): INTEGER;
VAR
  Num: INTEGER;
  BEGIN
  WHILE NOT (Dat[I] IN ['0'..'9']) AND (I <= LENGTH(Date)) DO
  I := I + 1;
  Num := 0;
  WHILE (Dat[I] IN ['0'..'9']) AND (I <= LENGTH(Date)) DO
    BEGIN
      Num := (ORD(Dat[I]) - ORD('0')) + (Num * 10);
      I := I + 1;
    END;
      Parsedate := Num;
    END;


  BEGIN
    Position := 1;
    Month := Parsedate(Position, Date);
    Day := Parsedate(Position, Date);
    Year := Parsedate(Position, Date) + 1900;

  END;


FUNCTION Caljul(M, D, Y: Integer): Real;
{Converts the integer month, day, and year to modified Julian date.}

VAR
  X: Real;


BEGIN
  X := INT(30.57 * M) + INT(365.25 * Y - 395.25) + D;
  IF M > 2 THEN
    IF INT(Y / 4) = Y / 4 THEN
      X := X - 1
```

Figure 7.4: The date utilities in the include file DATE.INC.

```
    ELSE
      X := X - 2;
  Caljul := X;
END;


PROCEDURE Julcal(X: Real; VAR Month, Day, Year: Integer);
{Converts the modified Julian value to the integer month, day, and year}

VAR
  M, D, Y: Real;
  D1: INTEGER;
BEGIN
  Y := INT(X / 365.26) + 1;
  D := X + INT(395.25 - 365.25 * Y);
  IF INT(Y / 4) * 4 = Y THEN
    D1 := 1
  ELSE
    D1 := 2;
  IF D > (91 - D1) THEN
    D := D + D1;
  M := INT(D / 30.57);
  D := D - INT(30.57 * M);
  IF M > 12 THEN
    BEGIN
      M := 1;
      Y := Y + 1;
    END;
  Month := TRUNC(M);
  Day := TRUNC(D);
  Year := TRUNC(Y);
END;


FUNCTION IntToDate(M, D, Y: INTEGER): DateStr;
{Converts three integer values to a standard date string.}

VAR
  I: INTEGER;
  Month, Day, Year: STRING [2];
  Date: Datestr;
BEGIN
  IF Y >= 1900 THEN
    Y := Y - 1900;
  STR(M: 2, Month);
  STR(D: 2, Day);
  STR(Y: 2, Year);
  Date := Month + '/' + Day + '/' + Year;
  FOR I := 1 TO LENGTH(Date) DO
    IF Date[I] = ' ' THEN
      Date[I] := '0';
  IntToDate := Date;
END;


FUNCTION DayOfWeek(Month, Day, Year: INTEGER): INTEGER;
{ Compute the day of the week using Zeller's Congruence. }
{ Sunday = 0 .. Saturday = 6 , year is actual year i.e. 1949}
```

Figure 7.4: (continued)

```
VAR
  Century: INTEGER;
BEGIN
  IF Month > 2 THEN
    Month := Month - 2
  ELSE
    BEGIN
      Month := Month + 10;
      Year := PRED(Year)
    END;
  Century := Year DIV 100;
  Year := Year MOD 100;
  DayOfWeek := (Day - 1 + ((13 * Month - 1) DIV 5) + (5 * Year DIV 4) +
                 Century DIV 4 - 2 * Century + 1) MOD 7
END;
```

Figure 7.4: (continued)

```
PROGRAM DateTest;

 {$I DATE.INC }

VAR
  Indate, Outdate: Datestr;
  Month, Day, Year, Wkday, M1, D1, Y1: INTEGER;
  Jul: REAL;

BEGIN
  WRITELN('Date I/O Test');
  WRITELN;
  WRITE('Enter date in MM/DD/YY format: ');
  READLN(Indate);
  DateToInt(Indate, Month, Day, Year);
  Wkday := DayOfWeek(Month, Day, Year);
  WRITELN;
  WRITELN(MonthArray[Month], ' ', Day, ', ', Year);
  WRITELN;
  WRITELN('That was a ', DayArray[Wkday], '.');
  WRITELN;
  WRITE('Integer values: ');
  WRITELN(Month, ' ', Day, ' ', Year);
  Jul := Caljul(Month, Day, Year);
  WRITELN;
  WRITE('Julian value: ');
  WRITELN(Jul: 6: 0);
  Julcal(Jul, M1, D1, Y1);
  WRITELN;
  WRITE('Integer values: ');
  WRITELN(M1, ' ', D1, ' ', Y1);
  Outdate := IntToDate(M1, D1, Y1);
  WRITELN;
  WRITE('String value: ');
  WRITELN(Outdate);
END.
```

Figure 7.5: A test program for the date utilities.

Days between Dates—NUMDAYS.PAS

The program *NUMDAYS.PAS* in Figure 7.6 uses the date routines to input two dates and compute the number of days between them. It shows again how a complex problem can be easily solved once a toolbox of routines has been developed.

```
PROGRAM Numdays;

{$I DATE.INC }

VAR
  Indate: Datestr;
  Month, Day, Year: INTEGER;
  Jul1, Jul2, Temp, Days: REAL;

BEGIN
  WRITELN('Days between dates');
  WRITELN;
  WRITE('Enter first date in MM/DD/YY format: ');
  READLN(Indate);
  DateToInt(Indate, Month, Day, Year);
  Jul1 := Caljul(Month, Day, Year);
  WRITELN;
  WRITE('Enter second date in MM/DD/YY format: ');
  READLN(Indate);
  DateToInt(Indate, Month, Day, Year);
  Jul2 := Caljul(Month, Day, Year);
  WRITELN;
  IF Jul1 > Jul2 THEN
    BEGIN
      Temp := Jul1;
      Jul1 := Jul2;
      Jul2 := Temp
    END;
  Days := Jul2 - Jul1;
  WRITELN('There are ', Days: 5: 0, ' days between the dates.')
END.
```

Figure 7.6: Program to calculate the number of days between dates.

More Screen I/O Routines—ROUTINE3.INC

The include file *ROUTINE3.INC*, listed in Figure 7.7, contains a few more subprograms to help create attractive and error-free user input and output.

Routines *DrawBox* and *ClrBox* are a little like the *WINDOW .INC* routines presented in Chapter 1, but they work on any version of Turbo Pascal, since they do not require the WINDOW command, available only in the IBM PC version of Turbo. *DrawBox* will draw a box on the screen using the user-specified characters. *ClrBox* will blank the area inside the box.

Procedure *GetStr* is used to get a valid input string from the keyboard within certain limitations. The maximum length of the string and the acceptable characters in the string are specified as calling parameters.

Function *Choice* is used with menus and CASE statements to write a prompt and then get a valid response from the keyboard. The prompt string, valid response character set, and screen row on which to display the prompt are parameters. This routine simplifies programs containing a number of menus.

Procedure *CenterScr* centers and writes a string on the specified row of the display screen. It is also useful for building menus and interactive screens.

```
TYPE
  Charset = SET OF CHAR;


PROCEDURE Drawbox(X1, Y1, X2, Y2: INTEGER;
                  Horiz, Vert: CHAR);
{ Draw a box on the screen from the top left (x1, y1) to the bottom
  right (x2, y2) using the specified characters. }

VAR
  I: INTEGER;
BEGIN
  GOTOXY(X1, Y1);
  FOR I := X1 TO X2 DO
    WRITE(Horiz);
  FOR I := SUCC(Y1) TO PRED(Y2) DO
    BEGIN
      GOTOXY(X1, I);
      WRITE(Vert);
      GOTOXY(X2, I);
      WRITE(Vert)
    END;
  GOTOXY(X1, Y2);
  FOR I := X1 TO X2 DO
    WRITE(Horiz)
END;


PROCEDURE Clrbox(X1, Y1, X2, Y2: INTEGER);
 { Erase interior of box, leave border alone }

VAR
  I: INTEGER;
BEGIN
  FOR I := SUCC(Y1) TO PRED(Y2) DO
    BEGIN
      GOTOXY(SUCC(X1), I);
      WRITE(' ': (X2 - X1 - 2))
    END
END;


PROCEDURE Getstr(VAR Inpstr: UniversalString;
                 Okset: Charset;
                 Maxlen: INTEGER);
 { Get a valid input string }

CONST
  Cr = ^M;
  Bs = ^H;

VAR
  Ch: CHAR;
  Getset: Charset;
BEGIN
  Inpstr := '';
  REPEAT
    IF LENGTH(Inpstr) < 1 THEN
      Getset := Okset + [Cr]
```

Figure 7.7: More useful screen and I/O utilities are contained in ROUTINE3.INC.

```
    ELSE IF LENGTH(Inpstr) < Maxlen THEN
      Getset := Okset + [Cr, Bs]
    ELSE
      Getset := [Cr, Bs];
    REPEAT
      Read(KBD, Ch)
    UNTIL Ch IN Getset;
    WRITE(Ch);
    IF Ch = Bs THEN
      BEGIN
        WRITE(' ' + Bs);
        Delete(Inpstr, LENGTH(Inpstr), 1)
      END
    ELSE IF Ch <> Cr THEN
      Inpstr := Inpstr + Ch
  UNTIL Ch = Cr
END;


FUNCTION Choice(Prompt: UniversalString;
                Term: Charset;
                Row: INTEGER): CHAR;

VAR
  Ch: CHAR;
BEGIN
  GOTOXY(1, Row);
  WRITE(Prompt, '? ');
  CLREOL;
  REPEAT
    READ(KBD, Ch);
    Ch := UPCASE(Ch)
  UNTIL Ch IN Term;
  WRITE(Ch);
  Choice := Ch
END;


PROCEDURE Centerscr(St: UniversalString;
                    Row: INTEGER);
{ Center string on CRT }
BEGIN
  GOTOXY((80 - LENGTH(St)) DIV 2, Row);
  WRITE(St)
END;
```

Figure 7.7: (continued)

A Perpetual Calendar Program—CALENDAR.PAS

The final program in this chapter, CALENDAR.PAS in Figure 7.8, "puts it all together" and uses routines from both the DATE.INC and ROUTINE3.INC libraries to create a "perpetual" calendar program. The calendar for any month and year in this century can be displayed on the screen just by entering the desired date.

```
PROGRAM Calendar;

 { Based on a bulletin board program by Steve Fox and William L. Mabee }

CONST
  Scrwid = 80;          { Number of columns on screen }
  Scrlen = 25;          { Number of rows on screen }
  Colspc = 5;           { Spacing between columns (characters)}
  Rowspc = 2;           { Spacing between rows (lines) }

VAR
  Ch: CHAR;
  Colbeg, Colend, Rowbeg, Rowend, Day, Month, Year: INTEGER;

  {$I ROUTINE.INC }
  {$I ROUTINE3.INC }


PROCEDURE Getdate;

CONST
  Digits: Charset = ['.', '-', '0'..'9', 'e', 'E'];

VAR
  Code: INTEGER;
  Prompt: UniversalString;
BEGIN
  Day := 1;

  REPEAT
    GOTOXY(1, PRED(SCRLEN));
    WRITE('Month number of desired calendar: ');
    CLREOL;
    GETSTR(Prompt, Digits, 2);
    VAL(Prompt, Month, Code)
  UNTIL (Code = 0) AND (Month IN [1..12]);

  REPEAT
    GOTOXY(40, PRED(SCRLEN));
    CLREOL;
    WRITE('Year: 19');
    GETSTR(Prompt, Digits, 2);
    VAL(Prompt, Year, Code)
  UNTIL Code = 0;
  Year := Year + 1900
END;


PROCEDURE Makecalendar;
{$I DATE.INC }

VAR
  I, Weekday, Numday: INTEGER;
  Yearstr: STRING [4];

BEGIN
  STR(Year, Yearstr);
  Centerscr('>>> ' + MonthArray[Trunc(Month)] + ' ' + Yearstr + ' <<<',
               Rowbeg);
```

Figure 7.8: A perpetual calendar program.

```
  GOTOXY(Colbeg, Rowbeg + Rowspc);
  FOR I := 0 TO 6 DO
    WRITE(Copy(Day_Array[I], 1, 3): Colspc);
  Weekday := Day_Of_Week(Month, Day, Year); { get weekday of first of
                                               month }
  Numday := Month_Days[Month]; { get number of days in month }
  IF (Month = 2) AND (Year MOD 4 = 0) THEN
    Numday := SUCC(Numday);
  FOR I := 1 TO Numday DO
    BEGIN
      GOTOXY(Colbeg + Colspc * ((Weekday + PRED(I)) MOD 7),
                  Rowbeg + Rowspc * ((Weekday + PRED(I)) DIV 7)
    + Rowspc * 2);
      WRITE(I: Colspc)
    END
END;

PROCEDURE Nextmonth;
BEGIN
  IF Month < 12 { check for December } THEN
    Month := SUCC(Month) { advance month }
  ELSE
    BEGIN
      Month := 1; { change it to January }
      Year := SUCC(Year) { advance year }
    END
END;


PROCEDURE Prevmonth;
BEGIN
  IF Month > 1 { check for January } THEN
    Month := PRED(Month) { subtract one month }
  ELSE
    BEGIN
      Month := 12; { change it to December }
      Year := PRED(Year) { subtract one year }
    END
  END;

BEGIN { main }
  Colbeg := (Scrwid - 7 * Colspc) DIV 2;
  Rowbeg := 4;
  Colend := Scrwid - Colbeg;
  Rowend := Rowbeg + 8 * Rowspc;
  CLRSCR;
  Getdate;
  Drawbox(Colbeg - 2, Rowbeg - 2, Colend + 2, Rowend, '*', '*');
  REPEAT
    Clrbox(PRED(Colbeg), PRED(Rowbeg), SUCC(Colend), Rowend);
    Makecalendar;
    Ch := Choice('A)nother Month, N)ext Month, P)revious Month, Q)uit ',
                 ['A', 'N', 'P', 'Q'], Pred(Scrlen));
    CASE Ch OF
      'A': Getdate;
      'N': Nextmonth;
      'P': Prevmonth;
    END
  UNTIL Ch = 'Q'
END.
```

Figure 7.8: (continued)

Conclusion

The ultimate test of the routines in this book is to take a common-place calculating application or file-manipulation procedure and see if you can put together a usable Turbo program in the same time it would have taken you to find the scratchpad and calculator on your desk (for the fourth time this morning). Try it, and prove to yourself that Turbo can honestly lay claim to being a useful tool in handling your daily business.

APPENDIXES A–K

A

Resources

Introduction

As Turbo becomes increasingly popular with students, experimenters, and developers of ambitious commercial applications, the range of resources related to this Pascal implementation becomes greater every day. Already, there is a growing collection of books on Turbo Pascal in addition to the classic presentations of standard Pascal. For those interested in Turbo, there are many good sources of additional information, support, and programming ideas.

Turbo Users' Groups

There is a large, national users' group that publishes an excellent newsletter, *TUG Lines,* which is filled with program listings, ideas, and problem work-arounds. The group is also assembling a program library and an all-Turbo bulletin board. It is entirely independent of Borland International and is everything that a good users' group should be. There is a nominal membership fee.

Turbo Users Group
Box 1510
Poulsbo, WA 98370

Local Groups

There are also an increasing number of local Turbo users' groups. They are generally affiliated with universities, or they function as special interest groups (SIGs) within larger computer clubs. Read the message section on local bulletin boards and inquire at local computer stores or colleges to find out about club activity in your area.

Borland SIG on CompuServe

CompuServe subscribers can join the Borland special interest group, which includes a forum and message board to communicate not only with other users, but with Borland personnel as well. There is a huge collection of programs available for use as-is or as springboards for further experimentation and development. Of course, as in any bulletin board system, the largest task is separating the genuinely useful programs from the rest.

CompuServe subscribers can access the SIG by typing

```
GO BOR
```

at any system prompt.

CompuServe, Inc.
5000 Arlington Centre Blvd.
Box 20212
Columbus, OH 43220

Bulletin Boards

Turbo-oriented bulletin boards have been springing up all over the country, and the "mainstream" IBM PC and CP/M-oriented boards have also been including more program listings in Turbo. Although any listing of bulletin boards is almost guaranteed to be out of date by the time it appears, the following list should be a start. Once you find one active board, you will always also find a listing of other currently-active boards posted on it.

BOSS BBS (NJ)	201-568-7293
Police Station BBS (NJ)	201-963-3115
Friel's BBS (IA)	319-266-8086
The Warehouse (OH)	513-258-0020
FIDO (Wilmington, DE)	302-764-7522

The best Turbo board in America is run by David Carroll, who is also one of the world's leading microcomputer authors and Turbo wizards. His board is at 209-296-3534.

B

Bibliography

Further Reading

However useful bulletin boards and clubs may be, the printed word remains the best source of ideas. Books not only contain collections of time-proven classic algorithms, but they are still about the only program resource that adds explanation and clarification to program listings.

Turbo-Specific Books

For the Turbo programmer there is a growing collection of Turbo-oriented books to save you from the task of converting other dialects into Turbo for many useful routines and programs. Some titles are listed below.

Carroll, David W. *Programming with Turbo Pascal,* Berkeley, Calif.: McGraw-Hill, 1985.

Duntemann, Jeff. *Complete Turbo Pascal,* Glenview, Ill.: Scott, Foresman, 1985.

Stivison, Douglas S. *Mastering Turbo Pascal,* Berkeley, Calif.: SYBEX, 1985.

Wood, Steve. *Using Turbo Pascal,* Berkeley, Calif.: Osborne McGraw-Hill, 1985.

Zaks, Rodnay. *Introduction to Pascal: Including Turbo Pascal™,* Berkeley, Calif.: SYBEX, 1986.

General Pascal and Programming Books

The Pascal language has long been one of the most widely written-about microcomputer topics. The following titles, most of which predate the Turbo dialect, are of interest to all Pascal programmers. One book is included to help advanced programmers expand into assembly language, and another will help beginners understand the logic behind computer programming.

Hergert, Douglas and Kalash, Joseph T. *Apple Pascal Games.* Berkeley, Calif.: SYBEX, 1981.

As noted in the text, this is still the most popular reference for game programming in all dialects of Pascal.

Hergert, Richard and Hergert, Douglas. *Doing Business with Pascal.* Berkeley, Calif.: SYBEX, 1983.

Excellent examples of Pascal structures applied to the solution of real-world problems. This is a gold mine of practical ideas that are even better suited to Turbo than to the UCSD Pascal in which the book was written.

Hunter, Bruce H. *Fifty Pascal Programs.* Berkeley, Calif.: SYBEX, 1984.

Kernighan, Brian W. and Plauger, P. J. *Software Tools in Pascal.* Reading, Mass.: Addison-Wesley, 1981.

This is a generic Pascal edition (the original was written for C) of one of the best books ever on real-world programming. Turbo versions of all the example programs are commonly available on bulletin boards and from clubs. For anyone attempting any serious programming project, this book—by two names synonymous with the concept of structured programming—is essential.

Ledgard, Henry and Singer, Andrew. *Elementary Pascal.* New York: Vintage, 1982.

The fundamental concepts of Pascal explained in the enjoyable context of Sherlock Holmes and Dr. Watson. This very readable book is particularly appropriate to Turbo enthusiasts because all program examples use a simplified generic dialect of Pascal. It is an enjoyable challenge to try to create working implementations of "Holmes's" programs in Turbo.

Ledgard, Henry; Singer, Andrew; and McQuaid, E. Patrick. *From Baker Street To Binary.* New York: McGraw-Hill, 1983.

This book contains an exploration of the fundamental concepts of computers and computer programming, as explained to Dr. Watson by Sherlock Holmes.

Scanlon, Leo J. *IBM PC Assembly Language: A Guide for Programmers.* Bowie, Md.: Brady, 1983.

Although Turbo Pascal is not even mentioned in the text, this is one of the clearest and most complete explorations of the operation of BIOS and BDOS functions. As such, it will be particularly useful to the programmer interested in exploring the use of the MSDOS and INTR procedures. It is much clearer and more readable than the standard IBM documentation. And for the Turbo programmer wishing to use in-line machine code, this is an excellent reference on the arcane art of assembly-language programming.

Zaks, Rodnay. *Introduction to Pascal (Including UCSD Pascal™)*. Berkeley, Calif.: SYBEX, 1981.

The original version of what is absolutely the best book on Pascal programming in the microcomputer world.

Books about Writing Adventure Games

Perhaps no other programming language is as ideally suited to writing text adventure games as Turbo. For those interested in pursuing this programming niche, there are several good books.

DaCosta, Frank. *Writing BASIC Adventure Programs for the TRS-80*. Blue Ridge Summit, Penna.: Tab, 1982.

Although specific to the dialect of BASIC used on the TRS-80, this book is still a good source for ideas on the structuring of adventure games.

Horn, Delton T. *Golden Flutes & Great Escapes*. Beaverton, Ore.: dilithium Press, 1984.

Although it is also oriented towards TRS-80 BASIC, this book contains many good ideas for adding depth and complexity to more ambitious adventures.

Liddil, Robert (editor). *The Captain 80 Book of BASIC Adventures*. Tacoma, Wash.: 80-Northwest Publishing, 1981.

Besides a listing of 18 of the classic BASIC adventures, this hard-to-find book also includes intriguing background on developing adventure ideas. All the code in the book, however, is entirely TRS-80 specific with a heavy reliance on PEEKs and POKEs, which are almost impossible to translate.

McGath, Gary. *COMPUTE!'s Guide to Adventure Games*. Greensboro, N.C.: Compute! Publications, 1984.

A nice overview of the history and attraction of adventure games and a simple explanation of how a generic adventure would be written.

Vile, Richard C. *Programming Your Own Adventure Games in Pascal*. Blue Ridge Summit, Penna.: TAB, 1984.

The best book on the topic. It is an easy task to convert the few UCSD-specific features to Turbo, and the explanations of

Pascal data structures and the construction of command parsers in Pascal are excellent. The program listings are fine examples of polished programming.

Periodicals

In addition to books, most of the popular computer magazines, including *Byte*, and *PC Magazine*, carry occasional articles on Turbo Pascal. Even more frequently, excellent articles on Turbo, as well as general programming topics, appear in:

Dr. Dobb's Journal, 2464 Embarcadero Way, Palo Alto, CA 94303.

PC Tech Journal, The World Trade Center, Suite 211, Baltimore, MD 21202.

The Computer Journal, 190 Sullivan Crossroad, Columbia Falls, MT 59912.

C

Pascal Operators

STANDARD PASCAL OPERATORS

	TYPE	FUNCTION	TYPE OF OPERAND(S)	TYPE OF RESULT
:=		assignment	any except file	
+	arithmetic	unary plus	integer, real	integer, real
−	arithmetic	minus sign	integer, real	integer, real
+	arithmetic	addition	integer, real	integer, real
+	set	union	set	set
−	arithmetic	subtraction	integer, real	integer, real
−	set	difference	set	set
*	arithmetic	multiplication	integer, real	integer, real
*	set	intersection	set	set
DIV	arithmetic	integer division	integer	integer
/	arithmetic	real division	integer, real	real
MOD	arithmetic	modulus	integer	integer
=	relational	equality	scalar, set, string, pointer	Boolean
<>	relational	inequality	scalar, set, string, pointer	Boolean
<	relational	less than	scalar, string	Boolean
<=	relational	less than or equal to	scalar, string	Boolean
<=	relational	set inclusion	set	Boolean
>	relational	greater than	scalar, string	Boolean
>=	relational	greater than or equal to	scalar, string	Boolean
>=	relational	set inclusion	set	Boolean
IN	relational	set membership	scalar IN set	Boolean
AND	logical	and	Boolean	Boolean
NOT	logical	negation	Boolean	Boolean
OR	logical	or	Boolean	Boolean

TURBO PASCAL OPERATORS

	TYPE	FUNCTION	TYPE OF OPERAND(S)	TYPE OF RESULT
+	string	concatenation	string,char	string
XOR	logical	exclusive or	Boolean	Boolean

D

Reserved Words

RESERVED WORDS

AND	NIL
ARRAY	NOT
BEGIN	OF
CASE	OR
CONST	PACKED
DIV	PROCEDURE
DO	PROGRAM
DOWNTO	RECORD
ELSE	REPEAT
END	SET
FILE	THEN
FOR	TO
FUNCTION	TYPE
GOTO	UNTIL
IF	VAR
IN	WHILE
LABEL	WITH
MOD	

TURBO PASCAL RESERVED WORDS

ABSOLUTE	SHR
EXTERNAL	STRING
INLINE	XOR
OVERLAY	
SHL	

E

Standard Pascal Functions and Procedures

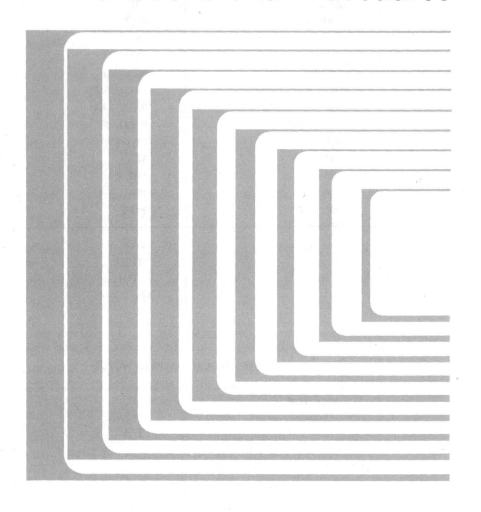

The italicized functions and procedures are not supported in Turbo Pascal.

FILE OPERATIONS	ARITHMETIC	PREDICATES
GET (F)	ABS (X)	EOF (F)
PAGE (F)	ARCTAN (X)	EOLN (F)
PUT (F)	COS (X)	ODD (X)
READ	EXP (X)	
READLN	LN (X)	
RESET (F)	SIN (X)	
REWRITE (F)	SQR (X)	
WRITE	SQRT (X)	
WRITELN		

TRANSFER	MEMORY MANAGEMENT	ORDERING
CHR (X)	*PACK (A,I,Z)*	PRED (X)
ORD (X)	*UNPACK (Z,A,I)*	SUCC (X)
ROUND (X)	NEW (P)	
	DISPOSE (P)	
TRUNC (X)	*NEW* $(P,T_1,\ldots T_N)$	
	DISPOSE $(P,T_1,T_2\ldots T_N)$	

F

Standard Identifiers included in Turbo Pascal

	CONSTANT	TYPE	FUNCTION	PROCEDURE	FILE
ABS			X		
ARCTAN			X		
BOOLEAN		X			
CHAR		X			
CHR			X		
COS			X		
EOF			X		
EOLN			X		
EXP			X		
FALSE	X				
INPUT					X
INTEGER		X			
LN			X		
MAXINT	X				
ODD			X		
ORD			X		
OUTPUT					X
PRED			X		
READ				X	
READLN				X	
REAL		X			
RESET				X	
REWRITE				X	
ROUND			X		
SIN			X		
SQR			X		
SQRT			X		
TEXT		X			
TRUE	X				
TRUNC			X		
WRITE				X	
WRITELN				X	

G

Operator Precedence

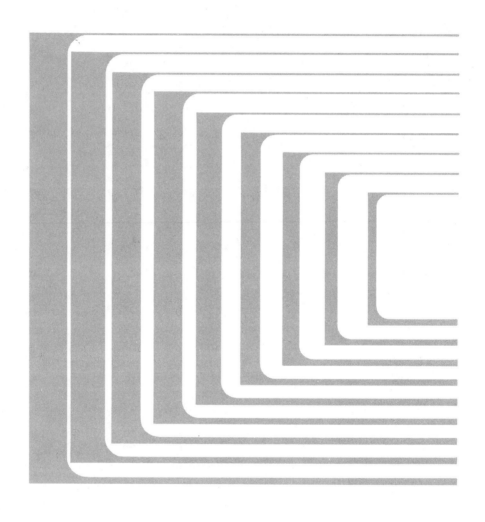

TURBO PASCAL PRECEDENCE

Level 3 (highest)	NOT
Level 2	* / DIV MOD AND
Level 1	+ − OR XOR (+ includes string concatenation)
Level 0	= < > <= >= <> IN

STANDARD PASCAL PRECEDENCE

Level 3 (highest)	NOT
Level 2	* / DIV MOD AND
Level 1	+ − OR
Level 0	= < > <= >= <> IN

H

ASCII Code

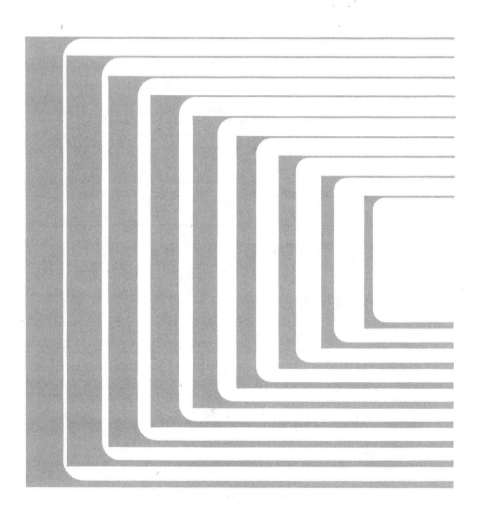

ASCII IN DECIMAL, OCTAL, HEXADECIMAL

#	OCTAL	HEX	CHAR	#	OCTAL	HEX	CHAR	#	OCTAL	HEX	CHAR	#	OCTAL	HEX	CHAR
0	000	00	NUL	32	040	20	SP	64	100	40	@	96	140	60	`
1	001	01	SOH	33	041	21	!	65	101	41	A	97	141	61	a
2	002	02	STX	34	042	22	"	66	102	42	B	98	142	62	b
3	003	03	ETX	35	043	23	#	67	103	43	C	99	143	63	c
4	004	04	EOT	36	044	24	$	68	104	44	D	100	144	64	d
5	005	05	ENQ	37	045	25	%	69	105	45	E	101	145	65	e
6	006	06	ACK	38	046	26	&	70	106	46	F	102	146	66	f
7	007	07	BEL	39	047	27	'	71	107	47	G	103	147	67	g
8	010	08	BS	40	050	28	(	72	110	48	H	104	150	68	h
9	011	09	HT	41	051	29	)	73	111	49	I	105	151	69	i
10	012	0A	LF	42	052	2A	*	74	112	4A	J	106	152	6A	j
11	013	0B	VT	43	053	2B	+	75	113	4B	K	107	153	6B	k
12	014	0C	FF	44	054	2C	,	76	114	4C	L	108	154	6C	l
13	015	0D	CR	45	055	2D	-	77	115	4D	M	109	155	6D	m
14	016	0E	SO	46	056	2E	.	78	116	4E	N	110	156	6E	n
15	017	0F	SI	47	057	2F	/	79	117	4F	O	111	157	6F	o
16	020	10	DLE	48	060	30	0	80	120	50	P	112	160	70	p
17	021	11	DC1	49	061	31	1	81	121	51	Q	113	161	71	q
18	022	12	DC2	50	062	32	2	82	122	52	R	114	162	72	r
19	023	13	DC3	51	063	33	3	83	123	53	S	115	163	73	s
20	024	14	DC4	52	064	34	4	84	124	54	T	116	164	74	t
21	025	15	NAK	53	065	35	5	85	125	55	U	117	165	75	u
22	026	16	SYN	54	066	36	6	86	126	56	V	118	166	76	v
23	027	17	ETB	55	067	37	7	87	127	57	W	119	167	77	w
24	030	18	CAN	56	070	38	8	88	130	58	X	120	170	78	x
25	031	19	EM	57	071	39	9	89	131	59	Y	121	171	79	y
26	032	1A	SUB	58	072	3A	:	90	132	5A	Z	122	172	7A	z
27	033	1B	ESC	59	073	3B	;	91	133	5B	[	123	173	7B	{
28	034	1C	FS	60	074	3C	<	92	134	5C	\	124	174	7C	¦
29	035	1D	GS	61	075	3D	=	93	135	5D	]	125	175	7D	}
30	036	1E	RS	62	076	3E	>	94	136	5E	↑	126	176	7E	~
31	037	1F	US	63	077	3F	?	95	137	5F	_	127	177	7F	DEL

Note: bit 7 (parity bit) is set to zero in this table.

THE ASCII SYMBOLS

NUL	— Null	VT	— Vertical Tabulation	CAN	— Cancel
SOH	— Start of Heading	FF	— Form Feed	EM	— End of Medium
STX	— Start of Text	CR	— Carriage Return	SUB	— Substitute
ETX	— End of Text	SO	— Shift Out	ESC	— Escape
EOT	— End of Transmission	SI	— Shift In	FS	— File Separator
ENQ	— Enquiry	DLE	— Data Link Escape	GS	— Group Separator
ACK	— Acknowledge	DC	— Device Control	RS	— Record Separator
BEL	— Bell	NAK	— Negative Acknowledge	US	— Unit Separator
BS	— Backspace	SYN	— Synchronous Idle	SP	— Space (Black)
HT	— Horizontal Tabulation	ETB	— End of Transmission Block	DEL	— Delete
LF	— Line Feed				

ASCII and Extended Graphics Codes

This section provides charts for the standard 128 character ASCII codes, and for the extended graphics codes available on the IBM PC and compatible computers. These screen graphics codes may be used in Turbo Pascal and some other IBM PC versions of Pascal.

The first extended character chart shows those characters available when using the WRITE and WRITELN statements with the CHR( ) procedure. The second table shows the characters available when accessing the IBM PC's screen memory directly. (For example, CHR(013) is a carriage return when used with WRITE and WRITELN, but the same code produces a music note when placed directly in screen memory.)

ASCII Value	Character	Control Character	ASCII Value	Character
000	(null)	NUL	032	(space)
001	☺	SOH	033	!
002	☻	STX	034	"
003	♥	ETX	035	#
004	♦	EOT	036	$
005	♣	ENQ	037	%
006	♠	ACK	038	&
007	(beep)	BEL	039	'
008	◘	BS	040	(
009	(tab)	HT	041	)
010	(line feed)	LF	042	*
011	(home)	VT	043	+
012	(form feed)	FF	044	,
013	(carriage return)	CR	045	-
014	♫	SO	046	.
015	☼	SI	047	/
016	►	DLE	048	0
017	◄	DC1	049	1
018	↕	DC2	050	2
019	‼	DC3	051	3
020	¶	DC4	052	4
021	§	NAK	053	5
022	▬	SYN	054	6
023	↨	ETB	055	7
024	↑	CAN	056	8
025	↓	EM	057	9
026	→	SUB	058	:
027	←	ESC	059	;
028	(cursor right)	FS	060	<
029	(cursor left)	GS	061	=
030	(cursor up)	RS	062	>
031	(cursor down)	US	063	?

ASCII Value	Character	ASCII Value	Character
064	@	096	`
065	A	097	a
066	B	098	b
067	C	099	c
068	D	100	d
069	E	101	e
070	F	102	f
071	G	103	g
072	H	104	h
073	I	105	i
074	J	106	j
075	K	107	k
076	L	108	l
077	M	109	m
078	N	110	n
079	O	111	o
080	P	112	p
081	Q	113	q
082	R	114	r
083	S	115	s
084	T	116	t
085	U	117	u
086	V	118	v
087	W	119	w
088	X	120	x
089	Y	121	y
090	Z	122	z
091	[	123	{
092	\	124	|
093	]	125	}
094	^	126	~
095	_	127	⌂

ASCII Value	Character	ASCII Value	Character
128	Ç	160	á
129	ü	161	í
130	é	162	ó
131	â	163	ú
132	ä	164	ñ
133	à	165	Ñ
134	å	166	ª
135	ç	167	º
136	ê	168	¿
137	ë	169	⌐
138	è	170	¬
139	ï	171	½
140	î	172	¼
141	ì	173	¡
142	Ä	174	«
143	Å	175	»
144	É	176	░
145	æ	177	▒
146	Æ	178	▓
147	ô	179	│
148	ö	180	┤
149	ò	181	╡
150	û	182	╢
151	ù	183	╖
152	ÿ	184	╕
153	Ö	185	╣
154	Ü	186	║
155	¢	187	╗
156	£	188	╝
157	¥	189	╜
158	Pt	190	╛
159	ƒ	191	┐

ASCII Value	Character	ASCII Value	Character
192	└	224	α
193	┴	225	β
194	┬	226	Γ
195	├	227	π
196	─	228	Σ
197	┼	229	σ
198	╞	230	μ
199	╟	231	τ
200	╚	232	Φ
201	╔	233	Θ
202	╩	234	Ω
203	╦	235	δ
204	╠	236	∞
205	═	237	Ø
206	╬	238	ε
207	╧	239	∩
208	╨	240	≡
209	╤	241	±
210	╥	242	≥
211	╙	243	≤
212	╘	244	⌠
213	╒	245	⌡
214	╓	246	÷
215	╫	247	≈
216	╪	248	°
217	┘	249	•
218	┌	250	·
219	█	251	√
220	▄	252	^{n}
221	▌	253	^{2}
222	▐	254	■
223	▀	255	(blank 'FF')

Character Set (00-7F) Quick Reference

DECIMAL VALUE	➡	0	16	32	48	64	80	96	112
⬇	HEXA DECIMAL VALUE	0	1	2	3	4	5	6	7
0	0	BLANK (NULL)	►	BLANK (SPACE)	0	@	P	‘	p
1	1	☺	◄	!	1	A	Q	a	q
2	2	☻	↕	"	2	B	R	b	r
3	3	♥	‼	#	3	C	S	c	s
4	4	♦	¶	$	4	D	T	d	t
5	5	♣	§	%	5	E	U	e	u
6	6	♠	▬	&	6	F	V	f	v
7	7	•	↨	'	7	G	W	g	w
8	8	◘	↑	(	8	H	X	h	x
9	9	○	↓	)	9	I	Y	i	y
10	A	◙	→	*	:	J	Z	j	z
11	B	♂	←	+	;	K	[	k	{
12	C	♀	∟	,	<	L	\	l	¦
13	D	♪	↔	—	=	M	]	m	}
14	E	♫	▲	.	>	N	^	n	~
15	F	☼	▼	/	?	O	_	o	△

Character Set (88-FF) Quick Reference

DECIMAL VALUE	➡	128	144	160	176	192	208	224	240
⬇	HEXA DECIMAL VALUE	8	9	A	B	C	D	E	F
0	0	Ç	É	á	░	└	╨	∝	≡
1	1	ü	æ	í	▒	┴	╤	β	±
2	2	é	Æ	ó	▓	┬	╥	Γ	≥
3	3	â	ô	ú	│	├	╙	π	≤
4	4	ä	ö	ñ	┤	─	╘	Σ	⌠
5	5	à	ò	Ñ	╡	┼	╒	σ	⌡
6	6	å	û	ª	╢	╞	╓	µ	÷
7	7	ç	ù	º	╖	╟	╫	τ	≈
8	8	ê	ÿ	¿	╕	╚	╪	Φ	°
9	9	ë	Ö	⌐	╣	╔	┘	Θ	•
10	A	è	Ü	¬	║	╩	┌	Ω	·
11	B	ï	¢	½	╗	╦	█	δ	√
12	C	î	£	¼	╝	╠	▄	∞	n
13	D	ì	¥	¡	╜	═	▌	ϕ	2
14	E	Ä	Pt	«	╛	╬	▐	∈	■
15	F	Å	ƒ	»	┐	╧	▀	∩	BLANK 'FF'

I

Turbo Syntax Diagrams

block

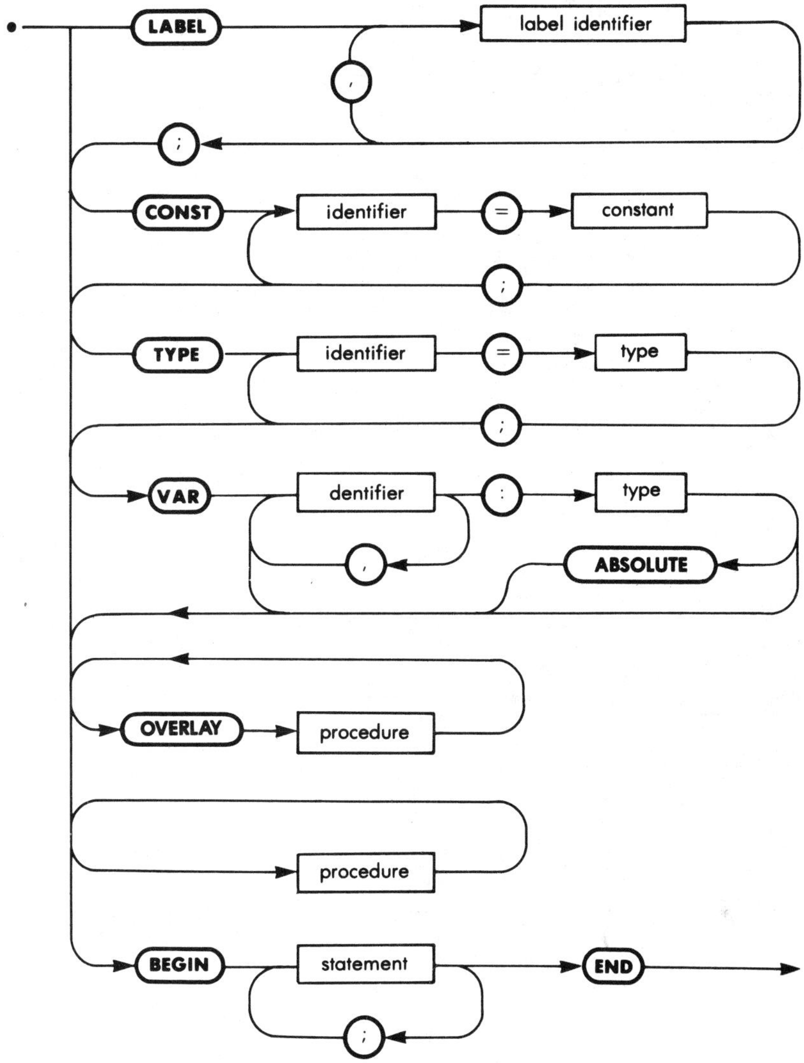
LABEL
label identifier
,
;
CONST
identifier
=
constant
;
TYPE
identifier
=
type
;
VAR
dentifier
:
type
,
ABSOLUTE
OVERLAY
procedure
procedure
BEGIN
statement
END
;

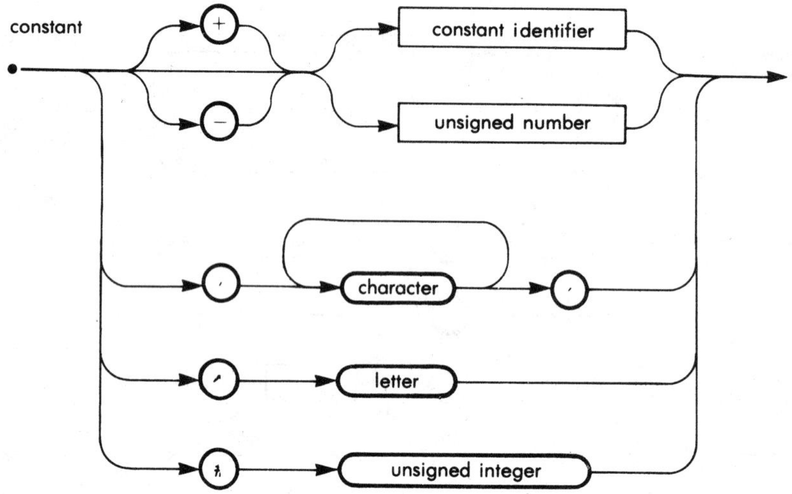
constant
+
−
constant identifier
unsigned number
'
character
'
letter
unsigned integer

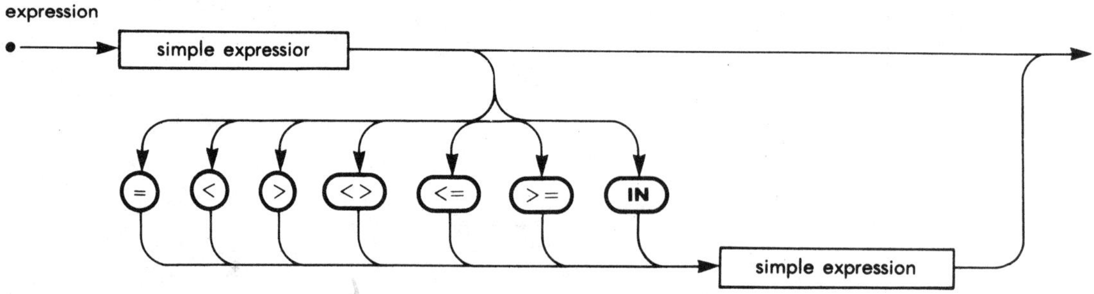
expression
simple expressior
=
<
>
<>
<=
>=
IN
simple expression

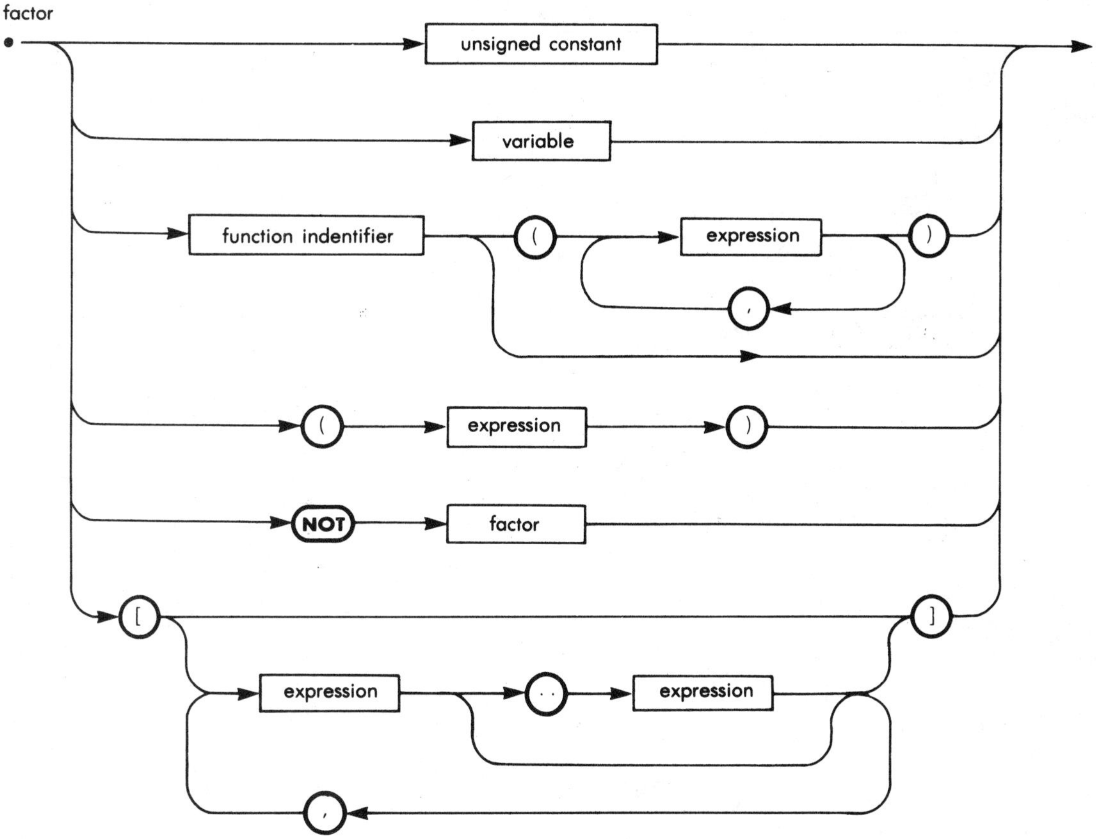
factor
unsigned constant
variable
function indentifier
(
expression
)
,
(
expression
)
NOT
factor
[
]
expression
..
expression
,

field list

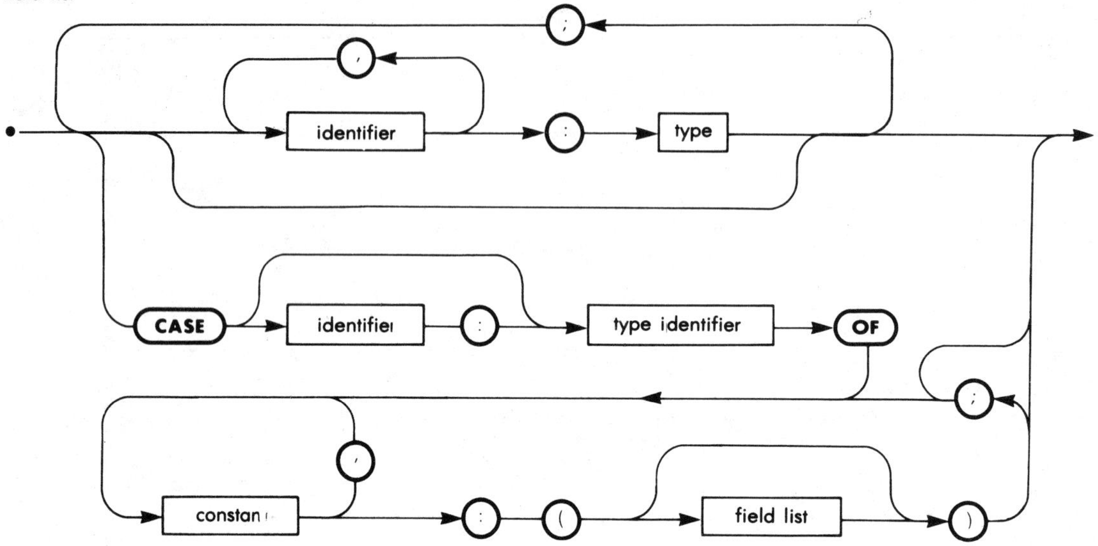

identifier

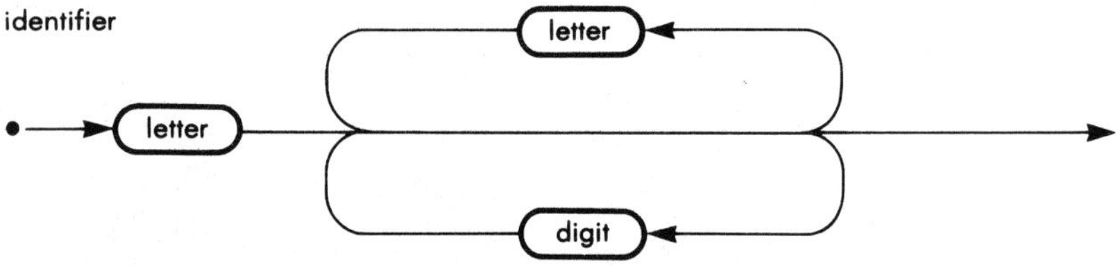

label identifier

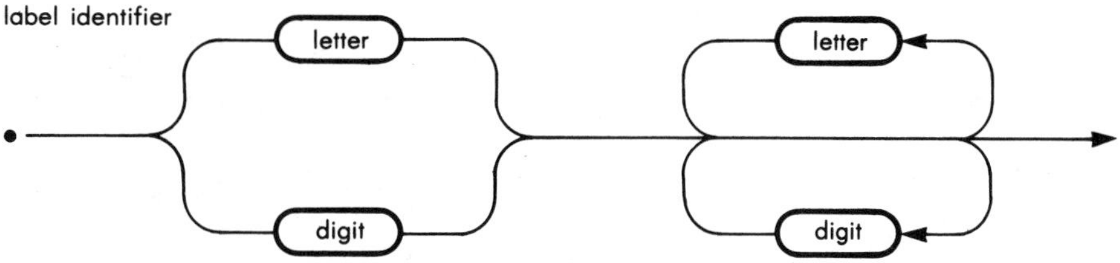

strin

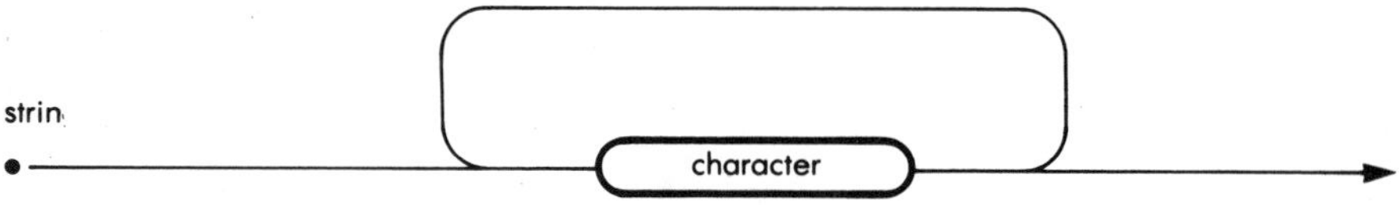

parameter list

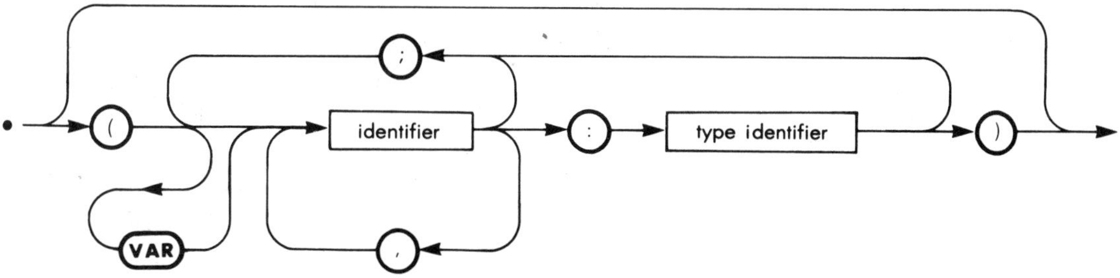

program

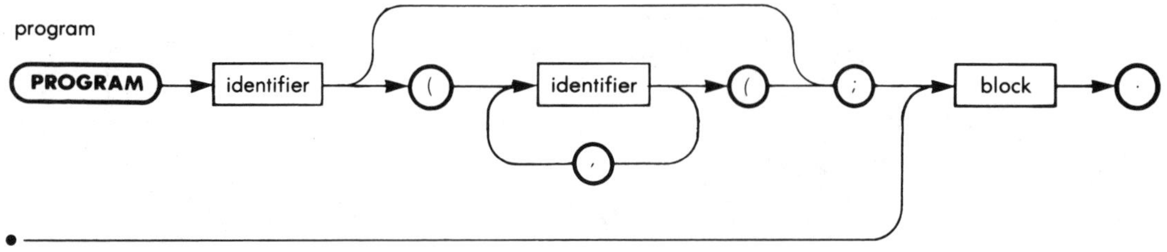

proce

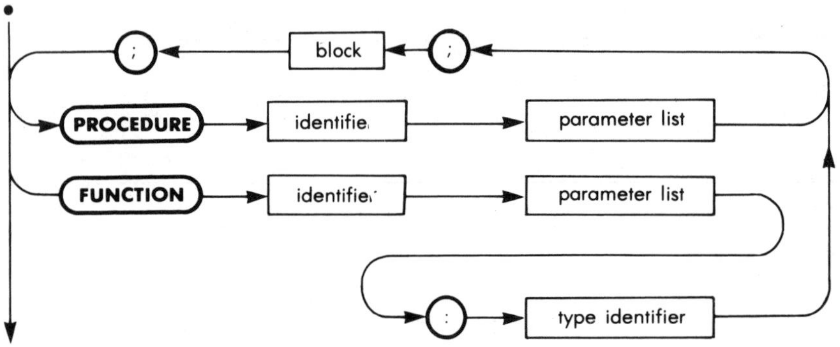

simple expression

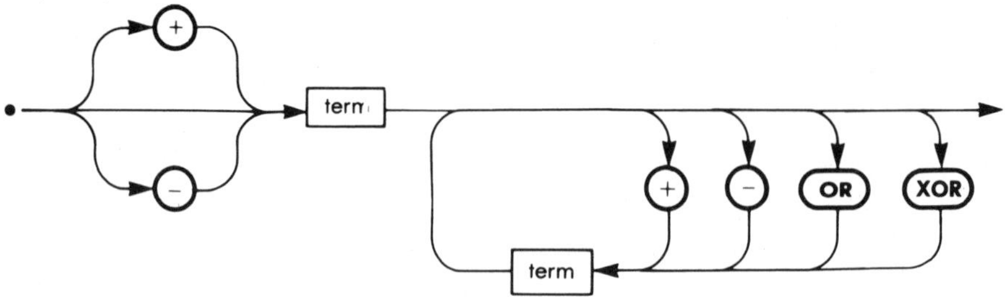

simple type

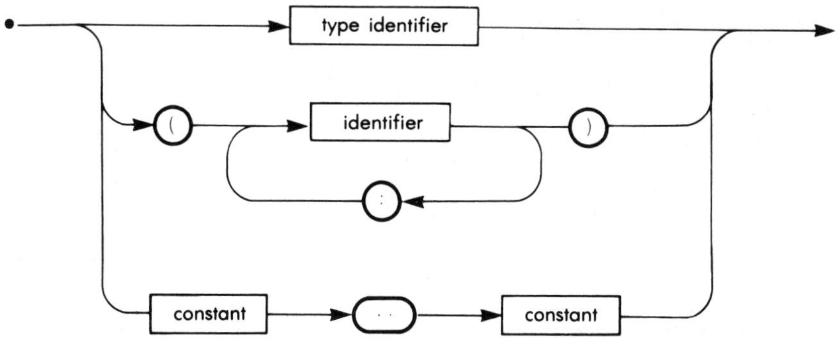

statement

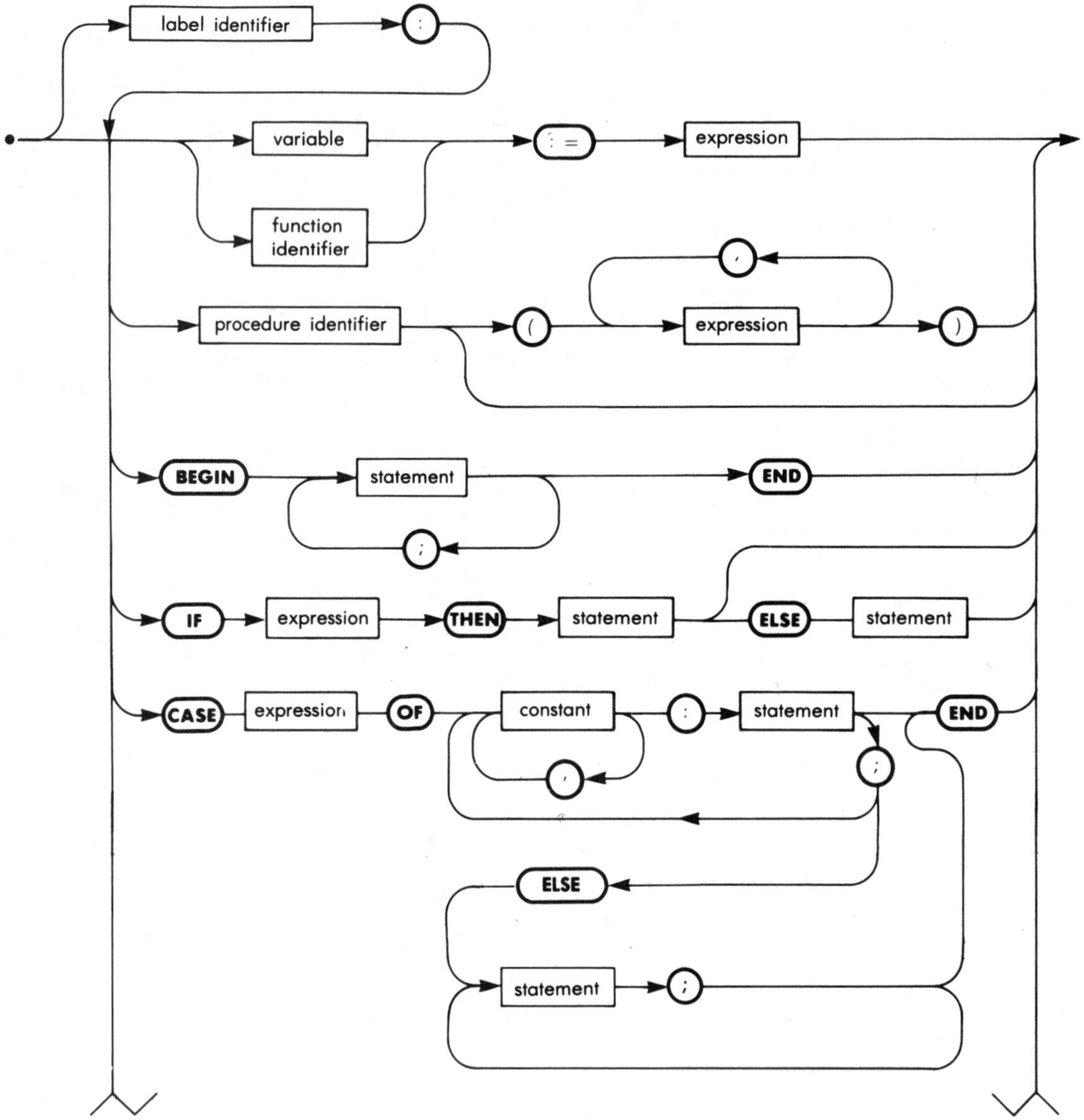
label identifier
:
variable
:=
expression
function
identifier
procedure identifier
(
,
expression
)
BEGIN
statement
;
END
IF
expression
THEN
statement
ELSE
statement
CASE
expression
OF
constant
,
:
statement
;
END
ELSE
statement
;

statement (cont.)

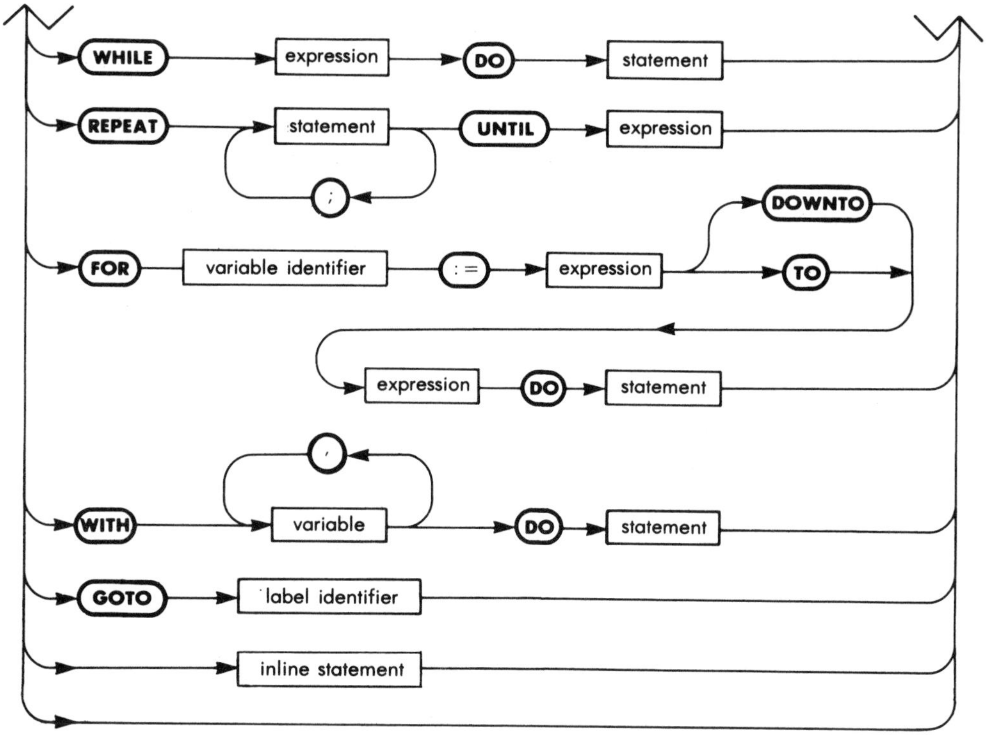

term

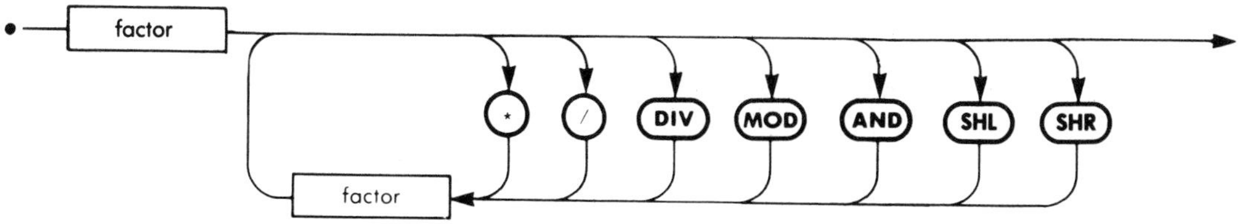

type

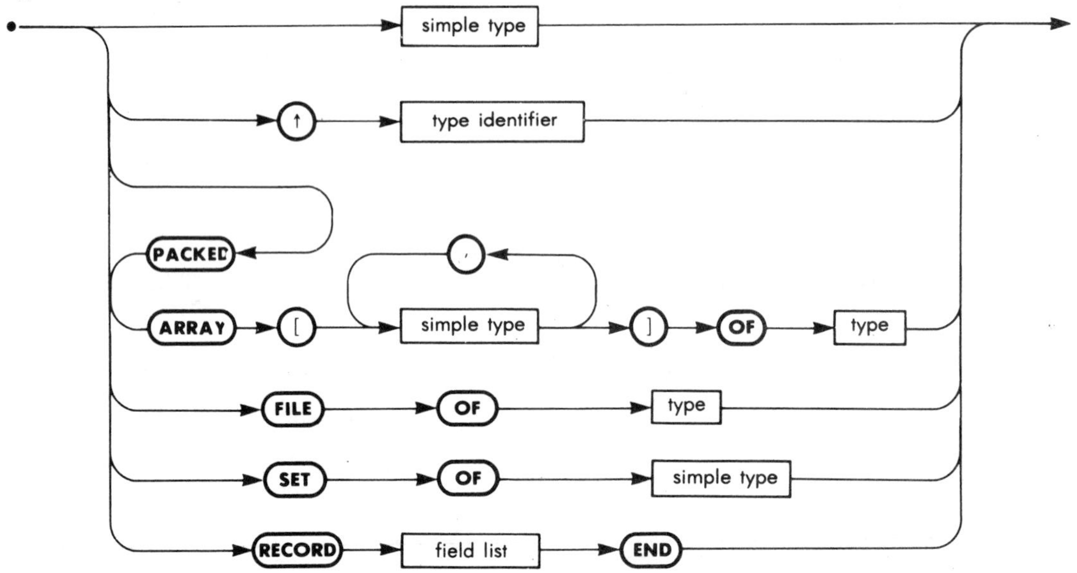

unsigned constant

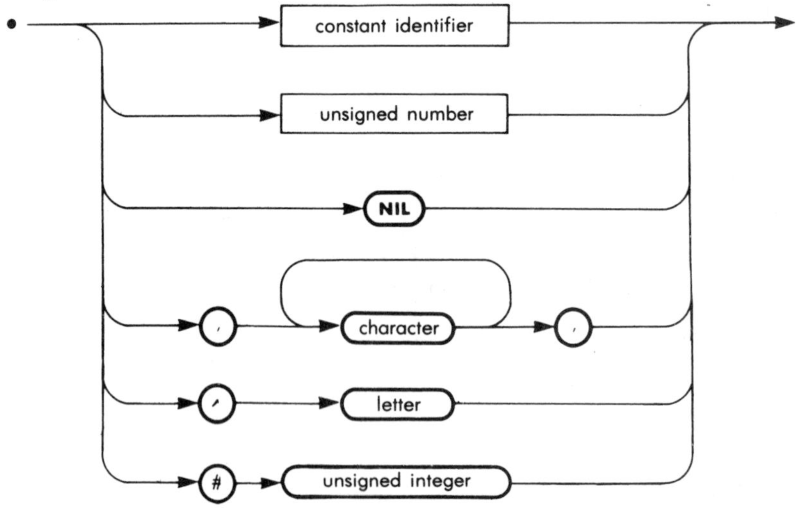

unsigned integer

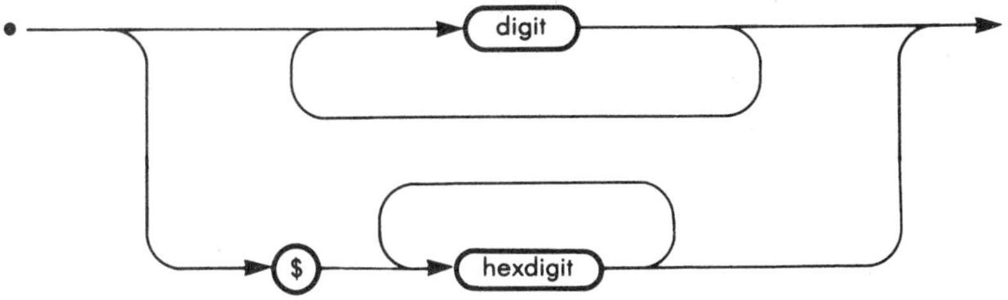

unsigned number

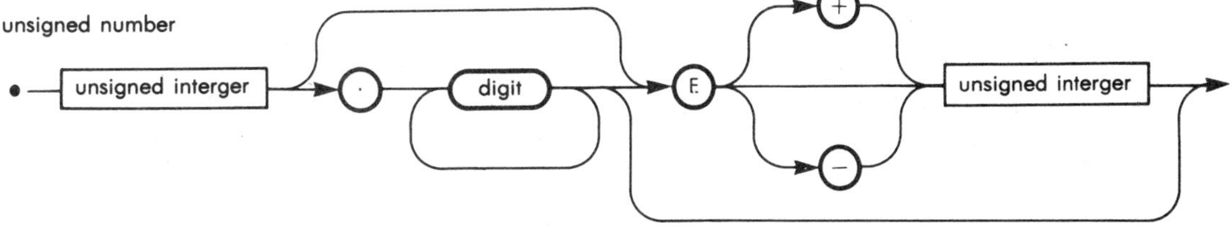

variable

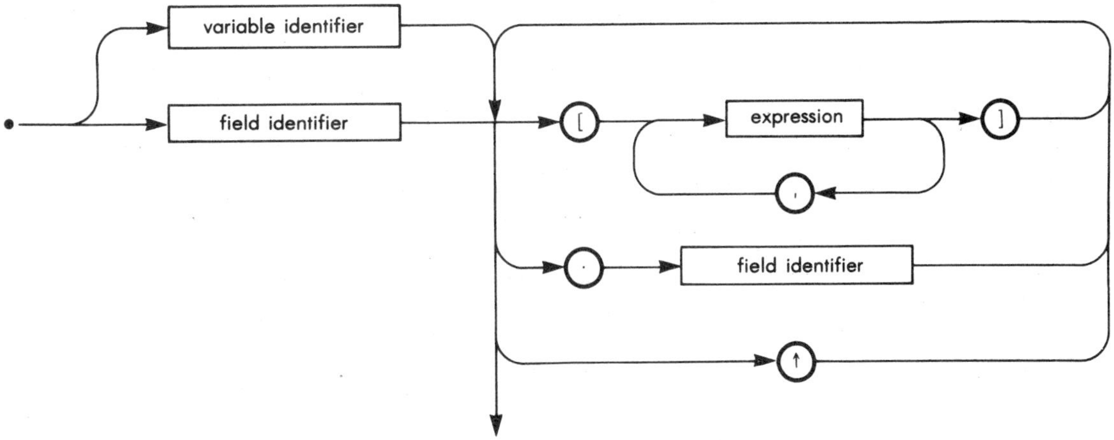

inline statement

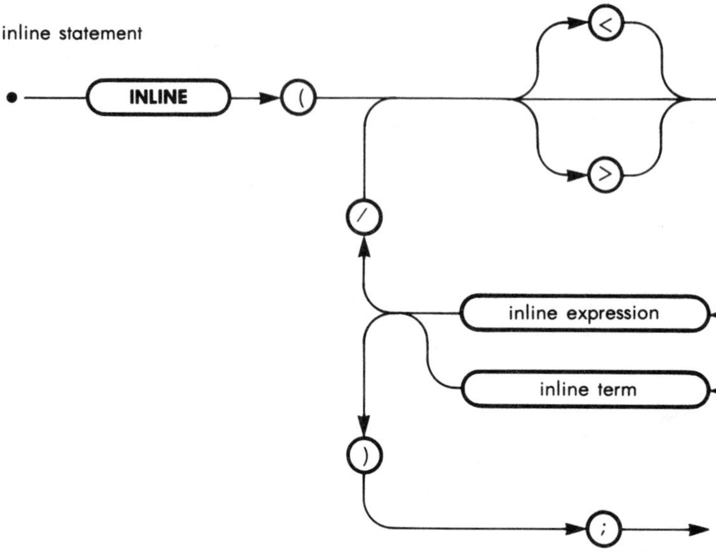

inline expression

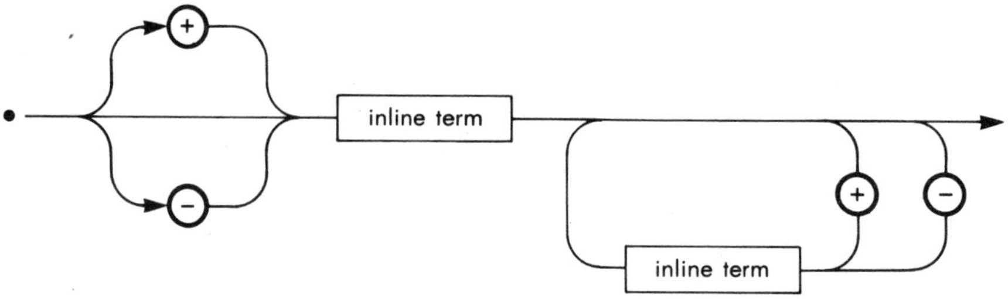

inline term

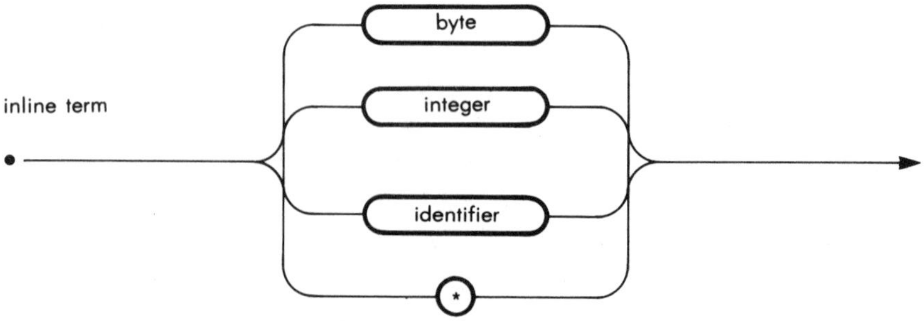

J

Usual Turbo Limitations

# characters in a	STRING	255
# elements in a	SET	256
Maximum value of a	REAL	1E+38, 11 digits
Minimum value of a	REAL	1E−38, 11 digits
Maximum nesting of	WITH	9
Maximum code size	BYTES	64K *
Maximum variable	BYTES	64K *
Maximum open	FILES	16 - MS/PC-DOS 2.0+

*CP/M 80 maximum 64k total for program and variables combined.

K

Turbo Pascal Reserved Functions and Procedures

INTRINSIC	TYPE	VERSION(S)
ADDR	FUNCTION	ALL
APPEND	PROCEDURE	3.0+
ASSIGN	PROCEDURE	ALL
AUX	STDFILE	ALL
AUXINPTR	SYSPTR	ALL
AUXOUTPTR	SYSPTR	ALL
BIOS	PROCEDURE	CP/M
BDOS	PROCEDURE	CP/M
BLACK	SYSCONST	IBM 2.0+
BLUE	SYSCONST	IBM 2.0+
BLOCKREAD	PROCEDURE	ALL
BLOCKWRITE	PROCEDURE	ALL
BROWN	SYSCONST	IBM 2.0+
BUFLEN	SYSVAR	ALL
BW40	SYSCONST	IBM 2.0+
BW80	SYSCONST	IBM 2.0+
BYTE	TYPE	ALL
C40	SYSCONST	IBM 2.0+
C80	SYSCONST	IBM 2.0+
CHAIN	PROCEDURE	ALL
CHDIR	PROCEDURE	IBM 3.0+
CLOSE	PROCEDURE	ALL
CLREOL	PROCEDURE	ALL
CLRSCR	PROCEDURE	ALL
CON	STDFILE	ALL
CONCAT	FUNCTION	ALL
CONINPTR	SYSPTR	ALL
CONOUTPTR	SYSPTR	ALL
CONSTPTR	SYSPTR	ALL
COPY	FUNCTION	ALL
CRTEXIT	PROCEDURE	ALL
CRTINIT	PROCEDURE	ALL
CSEG	FUNCTION	16-bit
CYAN	SYSCONST	IBM 2.0+
DARKGRAY	SYSCONST	IBM 2.0+
DELAY	PROCEDURE	ALL

INTRINSIC	TYPE	VERSION(S)
DELETE	PROCEDURE	ALL
DELLINE	PROCEDURE	ALL
DRAW	PROCEDURE	IBM 2.0+
DSEG	FUNCTION	16-bit
ERASE	PROCEDURE	ALL
EXECUTE	PROCEDURE	CP/M
EXIT	PROCEDURE	3.0+
FILEPOS	FUNCTION	MS/PC-DOS
FILESIZE	FUNCTION	MS/PC-DOS
FILLCHAR	PROCEDURE	ALL
FLUSH	PROCEDURE	MS/PC-DOS
FRAC	FUNCTION	ALL
FREEMEM	PROCEDURE	2.0+
GETDIR	PROCEDURE	IBM 3.0+
GETMEM	PROCEDURE	ALL
GOTOXY	PROCEDURE	ALL
GRAPHBACKGROUND	PROCEDURE	IBM 2.0+
GRAPHCOLORMODE	PROCEDURE	IBM 2.0+
GRAPHMODE	PROCEDURE	IBM 2.0+
GRAPHWINDOW	PROCEDURE	IBM 2.0+
GREEN	SYSCONST	IBM 2.0+
HALT	PROCEDURE	3.0+
HEAPPTR	SYSPTR	ALL
HI	FUNCTION	ALL
HIRES	PROCEDURE	IBM 2.0+
HIRESCOLOR	PROCEDURE	IBM 2.0+
INSERT	PROCEDURE	ALL
INSLINE	PROCEDURE	ALL
INTR	PROCEDURE	16-bit
IORESULT	SYSVAR	ALL
KBD	STDFILE	ALL
KEYPRESSED	FUNCTION	ALL
LENGTH	FUNCTION	ALL
LIGHTBLUE	SYSCONST	IBM 2.0+
LIGHTCYAN	SYSCONST	IBM 2.0+
LIGHTGRAY	SYSCONST	IBM 2.0+

INTRINSIC	TYPE	VERSION(S)
LIGHTGREEN	SYSCONST	IBM 2.0+
LIGHTMAGENTA	SYSCONST	IBM 2.0+
LIGHTRED	SYSCONST	IBM 2.0+
LO	FUNCTION	ALL
LONGFILESIZE	FUNCTION	IBM 3.0+
LONGFILEPOS	FUNCTION	IBM 3.0+
LONGSEEK	PROCEDURE	IBM 3.0+
LOWVIDEO	PROCEDURE	ALL
LST	STDFILE	ALL
LSTOUTPTR	STDPTR	ALL
MAGENTA	SYSCONST	IBM 2.0+
MARK	PROCEDURE	ALL
MAXAVAIL	FUNCTION	ALL
MEM	SYSARRAY	ALL
MEMAVAIL	FUNCTION	ALL
MEMW	SYSARRAY	16-bit
MKDIR	PROCEDURE	IBM 3.0+
MOVE	PROCEDURE	ALL
MSDOS	PROCEDURE	MS/PC-DOS
NORMVIDEO	PROCEDURE	ALL
NOSOUND	PROCEDURE	IBM 2.0+
OFS	FUNCTION	16-bit
OVRDRIVE	PROCEDURE	CP/M-86
OVRPATH	PROCEDURE	IBM 3.0+
PALETTE	PROCEDURE	IBM 2.0+
PARAMCOUNT	FUNCTION	3.0+
PARAMSTR	FUNCTION	3.0+
PI	SYSCONST	ALL
PLOT	PROCEDURE	ALL
PORT	SYSARRAY	ALL
PORTW	SYSARRAY	16-bit
POS	FUNCTION	ALL
PTR	FUNCTION	ALL
RANDOM	FUNCTION	ALL
RANDOMIZE	PROCEDURE	ALL
RED	SYSCONST	IBM 2.0+

INTRINSIC	TYPE	VERSION(S)
RELEASE	PROCEDURE	ALL
RENAME	PROCEDURE	ALL
RMDIR	PROCEDURE	IBM 3.0+
SEEK	PROCEDURE	MS/PC-DOS
SEG	FUNCTION	16-bit
SIZEOF	FUNCTION	ALL
SOUND	PROCEDURE	IBM 2.0+
SSEG	FUNCTION	16-bit
STR	PROCEDURE	ALL
SWAP	FUNCTION	ALL
TEXTBACKGROUND	PROCEDURE	IBM 2.0+
TEXTCOLOR	PROCEDURE	IBM 2.0+
TEXTMODE	PROCEDURE	IBM 2.0+
TRM	STDFILE	ALL
TRUNCATE	PROCEDURE	IBM 3.0+
UPCASE	FUNCTION	ALL
USR	STDFILE	ALL
USRINPTR	SYSPTR	ALL
USROUTPTR	SYSPTR	ALL
VAL	PROCEDURE	ALL
WHEREX	FUNCTION	2.0+
WHEREY	FUNCTION	2.0+
WHITE	SYSCONST	IBM 2.0+
WINDOW	PROCEDURE	2.0+
YELLOW	SYSCONST	IBM 2.0+

The list above does not include the Turtle Graphics and IBM Extended Graphics intrinsics in Turbo Pascal 3.0.

INDEX

Selections from The SYBEX Library

Languages

BASIC

YOUR FIRST BASIC PROGRAM
by Rodnay Zaks
182 pp., illustr. in color, Ref. 0-092
A "how-to-program" book for the first time computer user, aged 8 to 88.

FIFTY BASIC EXERCISES
by J. P. Lamoitier
232 pp., 90 illustr., Ref. 0-056
Teaches BASIC through actual practice, using graduated exercises drawn from everyday applications. Programs written in Microsoft BASIC.

BASIC FOR BUSINESS
by Douglas Hergert
224 pp., 15 illustr., Ref. 0-080
A logically organized, no-nonsense introduction to BASIC programming for business applications. Includes many fully-explained accounting programs, and shows you how to write your own.

EXECUTIVE PLANNING WITH BASIC
by X. T. Bui
196 pp., 19 illustr., Ref. 0-083
An important collection of business management decision models in BASIC, including inventory management (EOQ), critical path analysis and PERT, financial ratio analysis, portfolio management, and much more.

BASIC PROGRAMS FOR SCIENTISTS AND ENGINEERS
by Alan R. Miller
318 pp., 120 illustr., Ref. 0-073
This book from the "Programs for Scientists and Engineers" series provides a library of problem-solving programs while developing the reader's proficiency in BASIC.

Pascal

INTRODUCTION TO PASCAL (Including Turbo Pascal™)
by Rodnay Zaks
450 pp., illustr., Ref. 0-319-8
In Zaks' classic style that has already helped a quarter of a million people learn Pascal, and now in a version that features Turbo Pascal.

INTRODUCTION TO TURBO PASCAL
by Douglas Stivison
268 pp., illustr., Ref. 0-269-8
This bestseller enhances the unique aspects of Turbo Pascal by concentrating on the extended applications capabilities offered, while giving a full introductory tutorial.

INTRODUCTION TO PASCAL (Including UCSD Pascal™)
by Rodnay Zaks
420 pp., 130 illustr., Ref. 0-066
A step-by-step introduction for anyone who wants to learn the Pascal language. Describes UCSD and Standard Pascals. No technical background is assumed.

THE PASCAL HANDBOOK
by Jacques Tiberghien
486 pp., 270 illustr., Ref. 0-053
A dictionary of the Pascal language, defining every reserved word, operator, procedure, and function found in all major versions of Pascal.

APPLE® PASCAL GAMES
by Douglas Hergert and Joseph T. Kalash
372 pp., 40 illustr., Ref. 0-074

A collection of the most popular computer games in Pascal, challenging the reader not only to play but to investigate how games are implemented on the computer.

PASCAL PROGRAMS FOR SCIENTISTS AND ENGINEERS

by Alan R. Miller

374 pp., 120 illustr., Ref. 0-058

A comprehensive collection of frequently used algorithms for scientific and technical applications, programmed in Pascal. Includes programs for curve-fitting, integrals, statistical techniques, and more.

DOING BUSINESS WITH PASCAL

by Richard Hergert and Douglas Hergert

371 pp., illustr., Ref. 0-091

Practical tips for using Pascal programming in business. Covers design considerations, language extensions, and applications examples.

Other Languages

FORTRAN PROGRAMS FOR SCIENTISTS AND ENGINEERS

by Alan R. Miller

280 pp., 120 illustr., Ref. 0-082

This book from the "Programs for Scientists and Engineers" series provides a library of problem-solving programs while developing the reader's proficiency in FORTRAN.

UNDERSTANDING C

by Bruce H. Hunter

320 pp., Ref 0-123

Explains how to program in powerful C language for a variety of applications. Some programming experience assumed.

FIFTY PASCAL PROGRAMS

by Bruce H. Hunter

338 pp., illustr., Ref. 0-110

More than just a collection of useful programs! Structured programming techniques are emphasized and concepts such as data type creation and array manipulation are clearly illustrated.

Technical

Assembly Language

PROGRAMMING THE 6502

by Rodnay Zaks

386 pp., 160 illustr., Ref. 0-135

Assembly language programming for the 6502, from basic concepts to advanced data structures.

PROGRAMMING THE Z80®

by Rodnay Zaks

624 pp., 200 illustr., Ref. 0-069

A complete course in programming the Z80 microprocessor and a thorough introduction to assembly language.

PROGRAMMING THE 6809

by Rodnay Zaks and William Labiak

362 pp., 150 illustr., Ref. 0-078

This book explains how to program the 6809 microprocessor in assembly language. No prior programming knowledge required.

PROGRAMMING THE 8086™/8088™

by James W. Coffron

300 pp., illustr., Ref. 0-120

This book explains how to program the 8086 and 8088 microprocessors in assembly language. No prior programming knowledge required.

PROGRAMMING THE 68000™

by Steve Williams

250 pp., illustr., Ref. 0-133

This book introduces you to microprocessor operation, writing application programs, and the basics of I/O programming. Especially helpful for owners of the Apple Macintosh or Lisa.

Hardware

FROM CHIPS TO SYSTEMS: AN INTRODUCTION TO MICROPROCESSORS

by Rodnay Zaks

552 pp., 400 illustr., Ref. 0-063

A simple and comprehensive introduction to microprocessors from both a hardware and software standpoint: what they are, how they operate, how to assemble them into a complete system.

MICROPROCESSOR INTERFACING TECHNIQUES

by Rodnay Zaks and Austin Lesea

456 pp., 400 illustr., Ref. 0-029

Complete hardware and software interfacing techniques, including D to A conversion, peripherals, bus standards and troubleshooting.

THE RS-232 SOLUTION

by Joe Campbell

194 pp., illustr., Ref. 0-140

Finally, a book that will show you how to correctly interface your computer to any RS-232-C peripheral.

MASTERING SERIAL COMMUNICATIONS

by Joe Campbell

250 pp., illustr., Ref. 0-180

This sequel to ***The RS-232 Solution*** guides the reader to mastery of more complex interfacing techniques.

Operating Systems

SYSTEMS PROGRAMMING IN C

by David Smith

275 pp., illustr., Ref. 0-266

This intermediate text is written for the person who wants to get beyond the basics of C and capture its great efficiencies in space and time.

THE PROGRAMMER'S GUIDE TO UNIX SYSTEM V

by Chuck Hickev/Tim Levin

300 pp., illustr., Re.f 0-268

This book is a guide to all steps involved in setting up a typical programming task in a UNIX systems environment.

REAL WORLD UNIX™

by John D. Halamka

209 pp., Ref. 0-093

This book is written for the beginning and intermediate UNIX user in a practical, straightforward manner, with specific instructions given for many business applications.

Computer Specific

Apple II—Macintosh

THE PRO-DOS HANDBOOK

by Timothy Rice/Karen Rice

225 pp., illustr., Ref. 0-230

All Pro-DOS users, from beginning to advanced, will find this book packed with vital information. The book covers the basics, and then addresses itself to the Apple II user who needs to interface with Pro-DOS when programming in BASIC. Learn how Pro-DOS uses memory, and how it handles text files, binary files, graphics, and sound. Includes a chapter on machine language programming.

THE MACINTOSH™ TOOLBOX

by Huxham, Burnard, and Takatsuka

300 pp., illustr., Ref. 0-249

This tutorial on the advanced features of the Macintosh toolbox is an ideal companion to The Macintosh BASIC Handbook.

PROGRAMMING THE MACINTOSH™ IN ASSEMBLY LANGUAGE

by Steve Williams

400 pp., illustr., Ref. 0-263

Information, examples, and guidelines for programming the 68000 microprocessor are given, including details of its entire instruction set.

THE EASY GUIDE TO YOUR APPLE II®

by Joseph Kascmer

147 pp., illustr., Ref. 0-122

A friendly introduction to the Apple II, II plus, and the IIe.

BASIC EXERCISES FOR THE APPLE®

by J.P. Lamoitier

250 pp., 90 illustr., Ref. 0-084

Teaches Applesoft BASIC through actual practice, using graduated exercises drawn from everyday applications.

THE APPLE II® BASIC HANDBOOK

by Douglas Hergert

250 pp., illustr., Ref. 0-115

A complete listing with descriptions and instructive examples of each of the Apple II BASIC keywords and functions. A handy reference guide, organized like a dictionary.

APPLE II® BASIC PROGRAMS IN MINUTES

by Stanley R. Trost

150 pp., illustr., Ref. 0-121

A collection of ready-to-run programs for financial calculations, investment analysis, record keeping, and many more home and office applications. These programs can be entered on your Apple II plus or IIe in minutes!

YOUR FIRST APPLE II® PROGRAM

by Rodnay Zaks

182 pp., illustr., Ref. 0-136

This fully illustrated, easy-to-use introduction to Applesoft BASIC programming will have the reader programming in a matter of hours.

THE APPLE® CONNECTION

by James W. Coffron

264 pp., 120 illustr., Ref. 0-085

Teaches elementary interfacing and BASIC programming of the Apple for connection to external devices and household appliances.

THE BEST OF EDUCATIONAL SOFTWARE FOR APPLE II® COMPUTERS

by Gary G. Bitter, Ph.D. and Kay Gore

300 pp., Ref. 0-206

Here is a handy guide for parents and an invaluable reference for educators who must make decisions about software purchases.

YOUR SECOND APPLE II® PROGRAM

by Gary Lippman

250 pp., illustr., Ref. 0-208

The many colorful illustrations in this book make it a delight for children and fun for adults who are mastering programming on any of the Apple II line of computers, including the new IIc.

THE MACINTOSH™: A PRACTICAL GUIDE

by Joseph Caggiano

280 pp., illustr., Ref. 0-216

This easy-to-read guide takes you all the way from set-up to more advanced activities such as using Macwrite, Macpaint, and Multiplan.

MACINTOSH™ FOR COLLEGE STUDENTS

by Bryan Pfaffenberger

250 pp., illustr., Ref. 0-227

Find out how to give yourself an edge in the race to get papers in on time and prepare for exams. This book covers everything you need to know about how to use the Macintosh for college study.

Commodore 64/VIC-20

THE BEST OF COMMODORE 64™ SOFTWARE

by Thomas Blackadar

150 pp., illustr., Ref. 0-194

Save yourself time and frustration with this buyer's guide to Commodore 64 software. Find the best game, music, education, and home management programs on the market today.

YOUR FIRST COMMODORE 64™ PROGRAM

by Rodnay Zaks

182 pp., illustr., Ref. 0-172

You can learn to write simple programs without any prior knowledge of mathematics or computers! Guided by colorful illustrations and step-by-step instructions, you'll be constructing programs within an hour or two.

COMMODORE 64™ BASIC PROGRAMS IN MINUTES
by Stanley R. Trost
170 pp., illustr., Ref. 0-154
Here is a practical set of programs for business, finance, real estate, data analysis, record keeping, and educational applications.

GRAPHICS GUIDE TO THE COMMODORE 64™
by Charles Platt
261 pp., illustr., Ref. 0-138
This easy-to-understand book will appeal to anyone who wants to master the Commodore 64's powerful graphics features.

THE BEST OF EDUCATIONAL SOFTWARE FOR THE COMMODORE 64
by Gary G. Bitter, Ph.D. and Kay Gore
250 pp., Ref. 0-223
Here is a handy guide for parents and an indispensable reference for educators who must make decisions about software purchases for the Commodore 64.

COMMODORE 64™ FREE SOFTWARE
by Gary Phillips
300 pp., Ref. 0-201
Find out what "free software" is all about and how to find the specific programs you need.

YOUR SECOND COMMODORE 64™ PROGRAM
by Gary Lippman
240 pp., illustr., Ref. 0-152
A sequel to *Your First Commodore 64 Program*, this book follows the same patient, detailed approach and brings you to the next level of programming skill.

THE COMMODORE 64™ CONNECTION
by James W. Coffron
250 pp., illustr., Ref. 0-192
Learn to control lights, electricity, burglar alarm systems, and other non-computer devices with your Commodore 64.

PARENTS, KIDS, AND THE COMMODORE 64™
by Lynne Alper and Meg Holmberg
110 pp., illustr., Ref. 0-234
This book answers parents' questions about the educational possibilities of the Commodore 64.

CP/M Systems

THE CP/M® HANDBOOK
by Rodnay Zaks
320 pp., 100 illustr., Ref 0-048
An indispensable reference and guide to CP/M—the most widely-used operating system for small computers.

MASTERING CP/M®
by Alan R. Miller
398 pp., illustr., Ref. 0-068
For advanced CP/M users or systems programmers who want maximum use of the CP/M operating system . . . takes up where our *CP/M Handbook* leaves off.

THE BEST OF CP/M® SOFTWARE
by John D. Halamka
250 pp., Ref. 0-100
This book reviews tried-and-tested, commercially available software for your CP/M system.

THE CP/M PLUS™ HANDBOOK
by Alan R. Miller
250 pp., illustr., Ref. 0-158
This guide is easy for beginners to understand, yet contains valuable information for advanced users of CP/M Plus (Version 3).

IBM PC and Compatibles

THE ABC'S OF THE IBM® PC
by Joan Lasselle and Carol Ramsay
143 pp., illustr., Ref. 0-102
This book will take you through the first crucial steps in learning to use the IBM PC.

IBM PCjr

IBM® PC*jr*™ BASIC PROGRAMS IN MINUTES

by Stanley R. Trost

175 pp., illustr., Ref. 0-205

Here is a practical set of BASIC programs for business, financial, real estate, data analysis, record keeping, and educational applications, ready to enter on your PC*jr*.

THE COMPLETE GUIDE TO YOUR IBM® PC*jr*™

by Douglas Herbert

625 pp., illustr., Ref. 0-179

Learn to master the new hardware and DOS features that IBM has introduced with the PC*jr*. A fold-out reference poster is included.

THE EASY GUIDE TO YOUR IBM® PC*jr*™

by Thomas Blackadar

175 pp., illustr., Ref. 0-217

This jargon-free companion is designed to give you a practical working knowledge of your machine—no prior knowledge of computers or programming is needed.

BASIC EXERCISES FOR THE IBM® PC*jr*™

by J.P. Lamoitier

250 pp., illustr., Ref. 0-218

PC*jr* BASIC is easy when you learn by doing! The graduated exercises in this book were chosen for their educational value and application to a variety of fields.

TI 99/4A

THE BEST OF TI 99/4A™ CARTRIDGES

by Thomas Blackadar

150 pp., illustr., Ref. 0-137

Save yourself time and frustration when buying TI 99/4A software. This buyer's guide gives an overview of the best available programs, with information on how to set up the computer to run them.

YOUR FIRST TI 99/4A™ PROGRAM

by Rodnay Zaks

182 pp., illustr., Ref. 0-157

Colorfully illustrated, this book concentrates on the essentials of programming in a clear, entertaining fashion.

Timex

YOUR TIMEX/SINCLAIR 1000® AND ZX81™

by Douglas Hergert

159 pp., illustr., Ref. 0-099

This book explains the set-up, operation, and capabilities of the Timex/Sinclair 1000 and ZX81. Covers how to interface peripheral devices and introduces BASIC programming.

THE TIMEX/SINCLAIR 1000® BASIC HANDBOOK

by Douglas Hergert

170 pp., illustr., Ref. 0-113

This complete alphabetical listing with explanations and examples of each word in the T/S 1000 BASIC vocabulary will allow you quick, error-free programming of your T/S 1000.

TIMEX/SINCLAIR 1000® BASIC PROGRAMS IN MINUTES

by Stanley R. Trost

150 pp., illustr., Ref. 0-119

A collection of ready-to-run programs for financial calculations, investment analysis, record keeping, and many more home and office applications. These programs can be entered on your T/S 1000 in minutes!

MORE USES FOR YOUR TIMEX/SINCLAIR 1000® Astronomy on Your Computer

by Eric Burgess and Howard J. Burgess

176 pp., illustr., Ref. 0-112

Ready-to-run programs that turn your TV into a planetarium.

TRS-80

THE RADIO SHACK® NOTEBOOK COMPUTER

by Orson Kellogg

118 pp., illustr., Ref. 0-150

Whether you already have the Radio

Shack Model 100 notebook computer or are interested in buying one, this book will clearly explain what it can do for you.

YOUR COLOR COMPUTER
by Doug Mosher
350 pp., illustr., Ref. 0-097
Patience and humor guide the reader through purchasing, setting up, programming, and using the Radio Shack TRS-80 Color Computer. A complete introduction.

Atari

YOUR FIRST ATARI® PROGRAM
by Rodnay Zaks
182 pp., illustr., Ref. 0-130
This fully illustrated, easy-to-use introduction to ATARI BASIC programming will have the reader programming in a matter of hours.

BASIC EXERCISES FOR THE ATARI®
by J.P. Lamoitier
251 pp., illustr., Ref. 0-101
Teaches ATARI BASIC through actual practice, using graduated exercises drawn from everyday applications.

THE EASY GUIDE TO YOUR ATARI® 600XL/800XL
by Thomas Blackadar
175 pp., illustr., Ref. 0-125
This jargon-free companion will help you get started on the right foot with your new 600XL or 800XL ATARI computer.

ATARI® BASIC PROGRAMS IN MINUTES
by Stanley R. Trost
170 pp., illustr., Ref. 0-143
You can use this practical set of programs without any prior knowledge of BASIC! Application examples are taken from a wide variety of fields, including business, home management, and real estate.

YOUR SECOND ATARI® PROGRAM
by Gary Lippman
250 pp., illustr., Ref. 0-232
The many colorful illustrations in this book make it a delight for children and fun for adults who are mastering BASIC programming on the ATARI 400, 800, or XL series computers.

Coleco

WORD PROCESSING WITH YOUR COLECO ADAM™
by Carole Jelen Alden
140 pp., illustr., Ref. 0-182
This is an in-depth tutorial covering the word processing system of the Adam.

THE EASY GUIDE TO YOUR COLECO ADAM™
by Thomas Blackadar
175 pp., illustr., Ref. 0-181
This quick reference guide shows you how to get started on your Coleco Adam using a minimum of technical jargon.

Software Specific

Spreadsheets

DOING BUSINESS WITH MULTIPLAN™
by Richard Allen King and Stanley R. Trost
250 pp., illustr., Ref. 0-148
This book will show you how using Multiplan can be nearly as easy as learning to use a pocket calculator. It presents a collection of templates for business applications.

DOING BUSINESS WITH SUPERCALC™
by Stanley R. Trost
248 pp., illustr., Ref. 0-095
Presents accounting and management planning applications—from financial statements to master budgets; from pricing models to investment strategies.

MULTIPLAN™ ON THE COMMODORE 64™
by Richard Allen King

260 pp., illustr., Ref. 0-231
This clear, straighforward guide will give you a firm grasp on Multiplan's functions, as well as provide a collection of useful template programs.

Word Processing

INTRODUCTION TO WORDSTAR®
by Arthur Naiman
202 pp., 30 illustr., Ref. 0-134
Makes it easy to learn WordStar, a powerful word processing program for personal computers.

PRACTICAL WORDSTAR® USES
by Julie Anne Arca
303 pp., illustr., Ref. 0-107
Pick your most time-consuming office tasks and this book will show you how to streamline them with WordStar.

THE COMPLETE GUIDE TO MULTIMATE™
by Carol Holcomb Dreger
250 pp., illustr., Ref. 0-229
A concise introduction to the many practical applications of this powerful word processing program.

THE THINKTANK™ BOOK
by Jonathan Kamin
200 pp., illustr., Ref. 0-224
Learn how the ThinkTank program can help you organize your thoughts, plans, and activities.

Data Base Management Systems

UNDERSTANDING dBASE III™
by Alan Simpson
250 pp., illustr., Ref. 0-267
For experienced dBASE II programmers, data base and program design are covered in detail; with many examples and illustrations.

UNDERSTANDING dBASE II™
by Alan Simpson
260 pp., illustr., Ref. 0-147
Learn programming techniques for mailing label systems, bookkeeping, and data management, as well as ways to interface dBASE II with other software systems.

ADVANCED TECHNIQUES in dBASE II™
by Alan Simpson
250 pp., illustr., Ref. 0-228
If you are an experienced dBASE II programmer and would like to begin customizing your own programs, this book is for you. It is a well-structured tutorial that offers programming techniques applicable to a wide variety of situations. Data base and program design are covered in detail, and the many examples and illustrations clarify the text.

Integrated Software

MASTERING SYMPHONY™
by Douglas Cobb
763 pp., illustr., Ref. 0-244
This bestselling book provides all the information you will need to put Symphony to work for you right away. Packed with practical models for the business user.

ANDERSEN'S SYMPHONY™ TIPS & TRICKS
by Dick Andersen
325 pp., illustr., Ref. 0-247
Organized as a reference tool, this book gives shortcuts for using Symphony commands and functions, with troubleshooting advice.

JAZZ ON THE MACINTOSH™
by Joseph Caggiano and Michael McCarthy
400 pp., illustr., Ref. 0-265
The complete tutorial on the ins and outs of the season's hottest software, with tips on integrating its functions into efficient business projects.

MASTERING FRAMEWORK™
by Doug Hergert
450 pp., illustr., Ref. 0-248

This tutorial guides the beginning user through all the functions and features of this integrated software package, geared to the business environment.

ADVANCED TECHNIQUES IN FRAMEWORK™

by Alan Simpson

250 pp., illustr., Ref. 0-267

In order to begin customizing your own models with Framework, you'll need a thorough knowledge of Fred programming languages, and this book provides this information in a complete, well-organized form.

ADVANCED BUSINESS MODELS WITH 1-2-3™

by Stanley R. Trost

250 pp., illustr., Ref. 0-159

If you are a business professional using the 1-2-3 software package, you will find the spreadsheet and graphics models provided in this book easy to use "as is" in everyday business situations.

THE ABC'S OF 1-2-3™

by Chris Gilbert and Laurie Williams

225 pp., illustr., Ref. 0-168

For those new to the LOTUS 1-2-3 program, this book offers step-by-step instructions in mastering its spreadsheet, data base, and graphing capabilities.

MASTERING APPLEWORKS™

by Elna Tymes

250 pp., illustr., Ref. 0-240

Here is a business-oriented introduction to AppleWorks, the new integrated software package from Apple. No experience with computers is assumed.

Computer Books for Kids

MONICA THE COMPUTER MOUSE

by Donna Bearden, illustrated by Brad W. Foster

64 pp., illustr., Hardcover, Ref. 0-214

Lavishly illustrated in color, this book tells the story of Monica the mouse, as she travels around to learn about several different kinds of computers and the jobs they can do. For ages 5–8.

POWER UP! KIDS' GUIDE TO THE APPLE IIe® /IIc™

by Marty DeJonghe and Caroline Earhart

200 pp., illustr., Ref. 0-212

Colorful illustrations and a friendly robot highlight this guide to the Apple IIe/IIc for kids 8–11.

BANK STREET WRITING WITH YOUR APPLE®

by Stanley Schatt, Ph.D. and Jane Abrams Schatt, M.A.

150 pp., illustr., Ref. 0-189

These engaging exercises show children aged 10–13 how to use Bank Street Writer for fun, profit, and school work.

POWER UP! KIDS' GUIDE TO THE COMMODORE 64™

by Marty DeJonghe and Caroline Earhart

192 pp., illustr., Ref. 0-188

Colorful illustrations and a friendly robot highlight this guide to the Commodore 64 for kids 8–11.

Humor

COMPUTER CRAZY

by Daniel Le Noury

100 pp., illustr., Ref. 0-173

No matter how you feel about computers, these cartoons will have you laughing about them.

MOTHER GOOSE YOUR COMPUTER: A GROWNUP'S GARDEN OF SILICON SATIRE

by Paul Panish and Anna Belle Panish, illustrated by Terry Small

96 pp., illustr., Ref. 0-198

This richly illustrated hardcover book uses parodies of familiar Mother Goose rhymes to satirize the world of high technology.

CONFESSIONS OF AN INFOMANIAC

by Elizabeth M. Ferrarini

215 pp., Ref. 0-186

This is one woman's tongue-in-cheek revelations of her pursuit of men, money, and machines. Learn about the many shopping services, information banks, and electronic dating bulletin boards available by computer.

THE SYBEX PERSONAL COMPUTER DICTIONARY

120 pp., Ref. 0-199

All the definitions and acronyms of microcomputer jargon defined in a handy pocket-sized edition. Includes translations of the most popular terms into ten languages.

Introduction to Computers

OVERCOMING COMPUTER FEAR

by Jeff Berner

112 pp., illustr., Ref. 0-145

This easy-going introduction to computers helps you separate the facts from the myths.

INTRODUCTION TO WORD PROCESSING

by Hal Glatzer

205 pp., 140 illustr., Ref. 0-076

Explains in plain language what a word processor can do, how it improves productivity, how to use a word processor and how to buy one wisely.

PARENTS, KIDS, AND COMPUTERS

by Lynne Alper and Meg Holmberg

145 pp., illustr., Ref. 0-151

This book answers your questions about the educational possibilities of home computers.

PROTECTING YOUR COMPUTER

by Rodnay Zaks

214 pp., 100 illustr., Ref. 0-239

The correct way to handle and care for all elements of a computer system, including what to do when something doesn't work.

YOUR FIRST COMPUTER

by Rodnay Zaks

258 pp., 150 illustr., Ref. 0-142

The most popular introduction to small computers and their peripherals: what they do and how to buy one.

Special Interest

COMPUTER POWER FOR YOUR LAW OFFICE

by Daniel Remer

142 pp., Ref. 0-109

How to use computers to reach peak productivity in your law office, simply and inexpensively.

THE COLLEGE STUDENT'S PERSONAL COMPUTER HANDBOOK

by Bryan Pfaffenberger

210 pp., illustr., Ref. 0-170

This friendly guide will aid students in selecting a computer system for college study, managing information in a college course, and writing research papers.

CELESTIAL BASIC

by Eric Burgess

300 pp., 65 illustr., Ref. 0-087

A collection of BASIC programs that rapidly complete the chores of typical astronomical computations. It's like having a planetarium in your own home! Displays apparent movement of stars, planets and meteor showers.

COMPUTER POWER FOR YOUR ACCOUNTING FIRM

by James Morgan, C.P.A.

250 pp., illustr., Ref. 0-164

This book is a convenient source of information about computerizing your accounting office, with an emphasis on hardware and software options.

SYBEX Computer Books are different.

Here is why . . .

At SYBEX, each book is designed with you in mind. Every manuscript is carefully selected and supervised by our editors, who are themselves computer experts. We publish the best authors, whose technical expertise is matched by an ability to write clearly and to communicate effectively. Programs are thoroughly tested for accuracy by our technical staff. Our computerized production department goes to great lengths to make sure that each book is well-designed.

In the pursuit of timeliness, SYBEX has achieved many publishing firsts. SYBEX was among the first to integrate personal computers used by authors and staff into the publishing process. SYBEX was the first to publish books on the CP/M operating system, microprocessor interfacing techniques, word processing, and many more topics.

Expertise in computers and dedication to the highest quality product have made SYBEX a world leader in computer book publishing. Translated into fourteen languages, SYBEX books have helped millions of people around the world to get the most from their computers. We hope we have helped you, too.

For a complete catalog of our publications:

SYBEX, Inc. 2344 Sixth Street, Berkeley, California 94710
Tel: (415) 848-8233 Telex: 336311

TURBO PASCAL LIBRARY

Programs on Disk

If you'd like to use the same programs in this book but don't want to type them in yourself, you can send for them on disk. The disk contains all the programs in the book on a Turbo Pascal compatible disk. To obtain this disk, complete the order form and return it along with a check or money order for $20.00.

Amador Computer Services
P.O. Box 699
Pine Grove, CA 95665

Name____________________________________

Address__________________________________

City/State/ZIP_____________________________

Enclosed is my check or money order.
(Make check payable to *Amador Computer Services.*)
Price includes applicable taxes and postage within the United States.

Turbo Pascal Library